IMAGES
of America

STAND-UP COMEDY
IN CHICAGO

Comedian James Wesley Jackson performs at the Gorton Community Center in Lake Forest, Illinois, in April 2010. (Courtesy of and photograph by Jimmy McHugh.)

ON THE COVER: Brian Schmidt performs at the Comedy Womb in the mid-1970s. (Courtesy of Chrissie Frey.)

IMAGES
of America

STAND-UP COMEDY
IN CHICAGO

Vince Vieceli and Bill Brady

ARCADIA
PUBLISHING

Published by Arcadia Publishing
Charleston, South Carolina

Printed in the United States of America

Library of Congress Control Number: 2013951874

For all general information, please contact Arcadia Publishing:
Telephone 843-853-2070
Fax 843-853-0044
E-mail sales@arcadiapublishing.com
For customer service and orders:
Toll-Free 1-888-313-2665

Visit us on the Internet at www.arcadiapublishing.com

This book is dedicated to every Chicago stand-up comedian who has ever had the courage to take the stage and tried to make strangers laugh, to every club owner and booker who has made a stage available to us, and to every Chicagoan, near and far, who has ever come to support us. Dying is easy; comedy is hard.

CONTENTS

ACKNOWLEDGMENTS

While we are incredibly grateful to every person or comedy club that provided photographs or assistance with this book, there are some whose contributions we must recognize.

Thank you to Kelsey Jones, Maggie Bullwinkel, and Arcadia Publishing for believing in the worthiness of this project as much as we did, and a heartfelt thanks goes to Eileen Barrett, Bette Brady, Sean Brady, and Megan Brady for their patience and understanding.

Special thanks to William Cramp for having the wisdom to understand you were capturing history, and the William Cramp Estate—especially Dr. Andrew Moorman and Pat Nowack—for sharing his work. A huge thank you goes to Gina Vieceli-Garza, Mike Ostrowski, Bob Rumba, and Jenna Dalgety, whose assistance we could not have done without.

Thanks goes to the following people, groups, and organizations for the hands, large and small, that they had in this project: Martin Bailon, Tina Beard, Lisa Bonnice, Bert Borth, Kay Cammon, Karen Conti, Tom Dreesen, Duck Logic, Sally Edwards, Chrissie Frey, Paul Frisbie, Bill Gorgo, Dave Grier, Monica Grier, Bert Haas, Ted Holum, Frank Hooper, Allan Johnson, Raymond Lambert, Pat McGann, Jimmy McHugh, Denise Mix, Ginger Frey Nicolaou, Jimmy Pardo, Marlene Patterson, Mike Preston, Pete Schwaba, Tom Senese, Mark Shufeldt, Mike Thomas, Ernie Tucker, Patti Vasquez, John Vieceli, Brad Wethern, Tracey Whitmer, Zanies Comedy Club, and the Harold Washington Library Center.

INTRODUCTION

While the bulk of these pages primarily focus on the years between 1970 and 1990, it would be incredibly disrespectful to ignore those who came before that period. After all, how can one write about stand-up comedy in Chicago without mentioning Jack Benny or Bob Newhart? Equal attention must be paid to comedians like George Carlin and Dick Gregory, whose tenure in Chicago considerably altered their careers. Overall, the "who's who" and "what's what" of Chicago stand-up comedy is such that the show biz cliche "without further introduction" must be disregarded as we provide a worthy primer on the subject.

In the early 20th century, there were primarily two sources of live comedy in Chicago. The first were plays staged at venues such as McVickers Theater and Hooley's Parlor Home of Comedy. Eddie Foy Sr., one of the first superstars of American comedy, was so respected that prior to an engagement in Chicago, those putting on his show honored his request to forgo a hotel and be put up in a furnished Lake Shore Drive home. Throughout the 1910s, Foy toured with his children as "Eddie Foy Sr. and the Seven Little Foys," a family vaudeville act. Foy is also remembered for his onstage attempts to calm Chicagoans during the deadly Iroquois Theater fire in 1903.

Chicagoans also got their live comedy via vaudeville shows, which contain the deepest roots of stand-up comedy. Taking the stage to the playing of "Fine and Dandy," comedy teams and monologists were audience favorites, although not all comedians began their careers that way. Waukegan native Jack Benny debuted as a serious violinist and was talented enough for Minnie Marx to suggest that he join the Marx Brothers as one of their touring musicians when Benny was still a teenager. It was not until the enlisted Benny was stationed at Naval Station Great Lakes during World War I that his comedic gift emerged.

Like Benny, Bob Hope and Edgar Bergen also debuted in vaudeville before adapting to new mediums. Raised in Cleveland, Hope entered vaudeville as half of a comedy song-and-dance duo before going solo and being selected to emcee vaudeville shows at Chicago's Stratford Theater. The Stratford engagement was originally for two weeks, but as Hope became a can't-miss funny man, he was retained for an additional six months.

Bergen doubled down on his career in the 1920s, commissioning Chicago carpenter Theodore Mack to create wisecracking dummy Charlie McCarthy, whose head alone cost the 16-year-old Bergen $35. His first performance was at the Waveland Avenue Congregational Church in Chicago, and soon after that, Bergen and McCarthy began to appear in vaudeville shows and short films. A recommendation from Noël Coward helped Bergen secure a guest appearance on Rudy Vallee's radio show, which led to a starring role on *The Chase and Sanborn Hour*. There, Bergen introduced a second dummy, Mortimer Snerd. Bergen was a fixture on the radio from 1937 until 1956.

The vaudevillian comedy team of Carroll and Isabelle Allen, parents of late-night television pioneer Steve Allen, are remembered less often. Sadly, Carroll died when Steve was 18 months old, after which Isabelle continued to perform under the name Belle Montrose and earned Milton Berle's praise as "the funniest woman in vaudeville." Young Steve applied what he had gathered from watching his mother's shows to become the class clown at several Chicago schools, including Hyde Park High School and St. Joseph Military Academy, a boarding school in nearby La Grange Park. A health issue prompted Allen's move to Arizona, where he entered radio and created a character named Claude Horribly that, years later, Allen said was "more or less an imitation of Bergen's Mortimer Snerd."

In addition to performing at vaudeville theaters, comedians also got stage time at speakeasies, including an Al Capone joint where a lit cigarette flung in Chicago native Morey Amsterdam's direction convinced him that Hollywood would be safer. The move paid off for Amsterdam, who starred on *The Morey Amsterdam Show* in the late 1940s before landing the role of Buddy Sorrell on *The Dick Van Dyke Show.*

Unlike Amsterdam, comedian Joe E. Lewis did not exit Chicago unscathed, and his 1927 engagement at the Green Mill later inspired the film *The Joker is Wild*, starring Frank Sinatra. Perhaps Milton Berle fared best. Berle confessed that once, between shows at the Oriental Theatre, the mob sped him to Cicero, where he performed for Capone and others at the Cotton Club.

In the 1950s, Chicago saw the emergence of four local talents who, despite their contributions, are often overlooked in the story of the area's comedy history.

Joe Conti's show business career began in 1936 when, at the age of 12, he tap-danced his way to first place in the Major Bowes' *Original Amateur Hour* talent contest. The victory scored Conti a talent contract, and the Detroit native soon began appearing in a string of Bowery Boys and Dead End Kids movies. Seeking a steadier living and hoping to remain in his adopted Chicago, Conti switched to comedy and found a home at Mangam's Chateau in suburban Lyons. From the 1950s to the 1970s, Conti performed at Mangam's with dancers, jugglers, acrobats, chorus lines, and emcees who sang. His engagement—perhaps the longest in Chicago (Joey Bishop is said to have performed for nearly a year at Chicago's Vine Gardens in the late 1940s)—reflected an era when nightclubs hired performers for several weeks, not just for the week or weekend. After Mangam's closed, Conti continued doing stand-up and won over a new generation of admirers. Conti, who died in 1997, was one of the few comedians who successfully transitioned from nightclubs to comedy clubs.

Far less cordial was insult comic Jack E. "Fat Jack" Leonard, whose sharp tongue warned others not to challenge him. Nightclub shows featuring Leonard, aka the "Sultan of Insult" and the "Mouth that Roared," were hot tickets thanks to his appearances with Jack Paar on *The Tonight Show.* The rotund, bald comic, who died in 1973 at age 63, arguably influenced Don Rickles.

The third forgotten comic is Fred Sheldon Greenfield, also known as Shecky Greene. Greene's comedy career began when he took a summer job at a Milwaukee resort and formed a comedy team with Sammy Shore, the club's social director. Their partnership did not last long, and Shore moved to Los Angeles, where, in 1972, he and his wife, Mitzi, opened a comedy club (which Mitzi later acquired in their divorce) that became the legendary Comedy Store. Greene saw greater success as a solo act, doing gigs in New Orleans and Miami nightclubs before landing in Las Vegas in 1953, where he performed for the majority of his career.

Perhaps Chicago's most forgotten comic is "Lonesome" George Gobel, Emmy-winning star of *The George Gobel Show*, which aired from 1954 to 1960, and, later, the proverbial funny man on *Hollywood Squares.* On both shows, Gobel plied the same unassuming, deadpan delivery that first had audiences laughing at Helsing's Vodvil Lounge, located near Sheridan Road and Montrose Avenue in Chicago.

Gobel is considered to be among those who influenced fellow Chicagoan Bob Newhart, a connection Newhart addressed in his 2006 biography, *I Shouldn't Even Be Doing This!: And Other Things That Strike Me as Funny*: "In the fifties I watched George Gobel," Newhart wrote. "He wasn't doing 'Take My Wife, Please.' He would just tell these neat little stories, like about how his wife, spooky little Alice, came up to him the other day. It was a softer, less aggressive brand of comedy." Newhart, of course, went on to star in *The Bob Newhart Show*, followed by *Newhart.*

The Chicago comedian to whom Newhart is more comparable is Shelley Berman, if only because the two routinely performed while seated and incorporated mock phone calls into their acts. Though he once wrote for *Tonight Starring Steve Allen*, Berman was an actor by trade and performed with the Compass Players in Chicago, which later became Second City. It was not until Berman saw Mort Sahl at Mister Kelly's in 1957 that he began transitioning to a solo act. Unlike Sahl, Berman stocked his act with one-man sketches and quickly rose through the comedy ranks until he suffered a career setback in 1963, when a television documentary showed the likeable comic reacting angrily to an phone ringing offstage during a performance.

With respect to all, no one was more responsible than Mort Sahl for the style of comedy practiced by stand-up comedians in and out of Chicago. Considered the father of modern stand-up, the Canadian-born, California-bred Sahl incorporated themes and punch lines from his own plays before replacing those bits with headlines—taken from that day's newspaper—that he referred to on stage. Sahl's performance style was different, too. What should have been a monologue felt more like a dialogue, and with Sahl donning a red cardigan sweater instead of a tuxedo, his shows surely came across as more personal.

One of Sahl's earliest Chicago performances occurred in 1954 at the Black Orchid—a performance that led *Chicago Tribune* critic Will Leonard to compare Sahl to Chicago's Washington Square Park orators: "[Sahl] pitches to the intelligentsia but dresses like a Bughouse Square orator in a rumpled sweater, an open collar shirt, and a haircut and shave that need redoing." If Leonard noticed the comedic ground Sahl was breaking, it was not played up nearly as much as Sahl's wardrobe. Three years later, Sahl's nonconformist attire was still newsworthy, as Leonard reported that "Mort Sahl hasn't embellished his act with a necktie yet, but his show this season is on a bigger scale than last." Others, however, did notice the cultural shift, if indirectly. In 1958, the *Chicago Tribune*'s Herb Lyon reported that college kids "jammed" Sahl's show at Mister Kelly's, and while ticket sales were strong, club owners were miffed at the "single-beer sipping" crowd.

Another equally impressive trait of Sahl's was that he often was the only comedian on the show, therefore it was his responsibility to warm up his own audience. By the time Budd Friedman, owner of the Improv, was introducing comedian after comedian (a practice called "showcasing") at his New York City club in the early 1960s, Sahl was already well established.

Bert Haas, executive vice president of Zanies Comedy Club, tells the story of booking Sahl into the downtown club and hearing Sahl confess that he had never performed with other comedians on the same bill. Somehow, Sahl, the father of modern stand-up, had completely missed the four-man shows (emcee, opener, feature, and headliner) of the early 1980s and the three-man lineups often employed today.

Ultimately, Sahl introduced distinctions within the comedy trade, separating himself from comedic actors like Eddie Foy, variety comedians like Milton Berle, and, as Second City emerged on the national stage, improvisational actors like John Belushi and Bill Murray (although when people learn that a stand-up comedian is from Chicago, it is not unusual for them to consequently ask if the comedian is affiliated with Second City).

Among Sahl's proteges was Lenny Bruce, who once quipped that Chicago was so corrupt that the cause of one's death could be, "He wouldn't listen." The so-called "sick" comedian played Chicago many times, but no performance was as famous as his Gate of Horn appearance in December 1962, when police halted the show and arrested Bruce, charging him with obscenity. Fellow comedian and Bruce's friend George Carlin, who had been sitting at an upstairs bar, inebriated, when the police arrived, was also arrested. Carlin was charged with disorderly conduct and later revealed that the Gate of Horn incident had a "radicalizing effect" on him.

In the early 1960s, Carlin briefly lived in Chicago. He was drawn to the city by, among other things, the Playboy Club, which opened in 1960 and offered steady pay and sophisticated entertainment. The Chicago Playboy Club was where St. Louis native Dick Gregory caught his big break, crossing over from the black audiences he frequently entertained at Chicago's Esquire Lounge and Regal Theater and at a nightclub he owned in south suburban Robbins. Gregory's Playboy Club opportunity arose in the early 1960s when comedian Professor Irwin Corey fell ill before a show and recommended Gregory, whom he had met previously. After Gregory's second set, *Playboy* founder Hugh Hefner offered the sociopolitical comedian a three-year contract starting at $250 per week for six weeks. The contract was just the type of pay and steady work many comedians sought during that era, and among the seekers were Chicago residents Tim Reid and Tom Dreesen, America's first black-and-white comedy team, who formed in 1969 and dubbed themselves Tim and Tom.

Tim and Tom quickly discovered what nearly every budding comedian in America already knew: they needed stage time—and lots of it—to develop and hone their act. To compensate, the pair practiced in front of a mirror and volunteered for charity events, social functions, and anything else that would get them before a live audience.

"We went to jazz clubs on the South Side of Chicago—Lurlean's and Lum's and places like that, where guys like Gene Ammons and Eddie Harris, these old jazz giants, would be—and we'd say, 'Do you guys mind if, when you take a break, we get up and do some routines?' And they did not mind. They were good ol' jazz guys," Dreesen said.

Tim and Tom even did a show in the yard at the Cook County Jail. Other performers on the show included Dizzy Gillespie, the Chi-Lites, and Billy Eckstine. Ironically, the act of Chicago comics gaining stage time in bizarre places did not stop after the arrival of full-time comedy clubs in the 1970s. With increasingly more comedians than spots in a show, savvy comics began finding, booking, and performing in non-comedy establishments willing to offer comedy shows once per week. Known as "one-nighters," the gigs populated the Chicago area, with perhaps the oddest gig held at the Stay Out All Night Disco in suburban Stone Park. There, comedy shows kicked off between 2:00 and 3:00 a.m.—but that is getting ahead of the story.

In time, the comedy team of Tim and Tom graduated to Rush Street clubs, like Punchinello's, and then the Playboy circuit. Each gig came with a catch, though—club owners hired them because their act was polished, so when they took the stage, there were few opportunities to work in new material; however, if they did not introduce new material, they risked the act getting stale. What Tim and Tom lacked was a stage where they could try out new material—or, as Reid reasoned, in order for them to be good, they needed a place to be bad.

The solution to the stage-time situation would have a domino effect on numerous people, and in some regards, that is what *Stand-Up Comedy in Chicago* is about. Yes, it is a compact history, but underneath that are the effects, repercussions, and reverberations of the first domino falling, with much of the resulting noise related to comedians.

Not all of the dominoes sounded alike, though; William Cramp's did not. To the Vietnam veteran, photography was a hobby, and his appearances at Chicago comedy clubs were only natural, friends say, since Cramp was happiest when taking pictures of smiling people. Many of the pictures included here were taken by Cramp. Without them, it is difficult to imagine this book ever being published. Sadly, Cramp passed away in 2012.

Hundreds of other photographs from personal collections were considered for this book, and while we paid attention to quality, we also recognized significance—that was the easy part. Because Chicago comics worked at a large number of local comedy clubs, and their points of entry into the scene varied, it was often difficult to assign a specific comic's photograph to a single chapter. In finalizing such decisions, we made our best efforts to consider a variety of criteria, including the quality of the available image, the year the comedian began, and the comedian's connection to a given club.

Omissions exist within this book, however, and the absence of a comedian or comedy club is not reflective of importance. In many cases, the inability to verify names, dates, or places forced us to disqualify some information from inclusion. Additional omissions occurred due to space constraints or a subject declining to participate.

In other cases, we were unable to uncover quality photographs—or any photographs. For instance, Cleveland native Arsenio Hall was living in Chicago and working the local comedy scene when he was selected to open for jazz singer Mary Wilson at a nearby venue. That booking helped launch his career, but images of Arsenio's Chicago days proved elusive.

We hope that what remains is a healthy, celebratory slice of one of the most underreported stories in Chicago's history.

One

Le Pub and the Comedy Cottage

In 1972, Tom Dreesen approached Henry Norton, owner of Le Pub on Chicago's Clark Street, and proposed an idea nearly as unconventional as Tim and Tom's act. One stand-up comedian after another would perform, Dreesen explained, just like at the Improv, Budd Friedman's place in New York. Norton, as owner of the Gate of Horn, understood the potential of live comedy, but he only offered Le Pub's slowest night: Monday. Dreesen promoted the first show heavily.

"When I got to Le Pub, there was a line around the block," said Dreesen, who then panicked when he realized that, to fill time, he would have to rely on comedians with whom he was unfamiliar.

"We pulled it off," Dreesen said. "Some acts got up, died like a dog or bombed, and some acts did very good. But it worked, and that became the first comedy club in Chicago."

Besides Tim and Tom, Le Pub performers included Jim Wiggins and two comedy teams—Daryl Bohannon and Brad Sanders and Jim O'Brien and Ken Sevara.

Advertised as the "Comedy Workshop," the shows attracted sizeable crowds until the shows ended in 1974, when Norton converted Le Pub into a gay bar and found that he no longer had slow nights. By then, Le Pub–inspired comedy shows were being offered elsewhere, including at the original Kingston Mines. Comedians (and brothers) Larry and Jim McManus were the men behind those shows, and during a chance visit to Rosemont in 1975, the brothers found a another venue perfect for hosting comedy—the Maroon Raccoon, owned by Edward "Big Ed" Hellenbrand.

That year, the McManus brothers started running the Comedy College show at the Maroon Raccoon five nights per week, utilizing Friedman's showcase format of comics, who each got an average of 10 minutes per set.

"Sometimes, 20 comedians would go up," Jim McManus said. While talent determined lineup placement, every comic was afforded the same amenities: spotlights fashioned from empty coffee cans and a stage made of wooden beverage crates with carpeting draped across them.

In time, the partnership between Raccoon owner Edward "Big Ed" Hellenbrand and the McManus brothers soured, with the brothers moving on as Hellenbrand turned the Maroon Raccoon into the Comedy Cottage. In 1986, the club's ownership was contested in a court case that involved Hellenbrand and his former general manager, Jay Berk, who ultimately gained control of the building and turned the venue into the Last Laff. Hellenbrand opened two Comedy Cottages in Rosemont and Roselle, with varying success, before exiting the comedy business in the early 1990s.

When speaking in Illinois schools as part of a Jaycees' youth drug prevention program in 1968, Tim Reid (left) and Tom Dreesen developed a rich chemistry that led them to form America's first interracial comedy team. The pair toured together for nearly five years before disbanding in 1974 when Reid moved to Hollywood. Reid starred in the television shows *WKRP in Cincinnati* and *Frank's Place*. (Courtesy of Tom Dreesen.)

Later, Dreesen moved west, too, where he lived out of an abandoned car, scraped by however he could, and completely devoted himself to stand-up. Long nights at the Comedy Store finally paid off in December 1975, when Dreesen made the first of his 60-plus *Tonight Show* appearances. Dreesen toured with Frank Sinatra for 13 years, performing as Sinatra's opening act. (Courtesy of Tom Dreesen.)

Influenced by Mort Sahl and other comedians he had watched at Mister Kelly's, Jim Wiggins was among the comics who took the stage at Le Pub's first show. Shown above performing at the Barrel of Laughs, Wiggins later shared a long friendship with George Carlin. As his career progressed, the gravelly-voiced Wiggins became the "Last Hippie in America." In November 2005, Wiggins made his *Tonight Show* debut at the age of 64, with host Jay Leno citing the Barrel of Laughs as one of Wiggins's regular stops. (Above, courtesy of Bill Brady, photograph by William Cramp; right, courtesy of Zanies Comedy Club.)

Class clowns at Marian Catholic High School, Jim O'Brien (left, light suit) and Ken Sevara rented tuxedos and talked their way past Playboy Club doormen just to watch O'Brien's friend Tom Dreesen perform with Tim Reid. With Dreesen mentoring them, the teenagers put together an act, toured colleges, and became the second-youngest performers on the Playboy circuit in the early 1970s. They also performed at the Hacienda Hotel in Las Vegas. In 1976, the pair moved west, where, at the Comedy Store, Mitzi Shore handpicked them to be the opening act for Richard Pryor, who was preparing for his album/film *Live on the Sunset Strip*. After they disbanded, O'Brien continued as part of another comedy team. Sevara followed the advice of Brenda Carlin, George's wife, and returned to Chicago, where he reinvented himself and became a successful stand-up. (Both, courtesy of Ken Sevara.)

At Le Pub, Tom Dreesen routinely reserved a place in the show for first-time comedians. It was called the virgin spot, and one night, he awarded it to South Side native Marsha Warfield, whose initial performance was so strong that Dreesen thought she had lied to him about being a first-timer. Warfield later found fame on the hit show *Night Court*, a sitcom created by Chicago native Reinhold Weege, which ran from 1984 to 1992. (Courtesy of Zanies.)

Initially part of the comedy team Bohannon and Sanders, Brad Sanders moved to Los Angeles in 1976 and has worked as a stand-up, actor, and writer ever since. He cocreated "It's Your World," a radio dramedy that aired on the *Tom Joyner Morning Show*, and starred as Clarence in the web series "The Clarence B&B Update" (an offshoot of the soap opera *The Bold and the Beautiful*), for which he earned two daytime Emmy nominations. (Courtesy of Brad Sanders.)

After Le Pub closed, Comedy Workshop shows were held at several Pickle Barrel locations in Chicago, with Jimmy Aleck (pictured) often serving as emcee. Aleck has appeared on *The Tonight Show* with Johnny Carson and Jay Leno and has written episodes for several television shows, including *According to Jim* and *Caroline in the City*. (Courtesy of Bill Brady; photograph by William Cramp.)

Beginning in 1975, one comedian whom Jimmy Aleck regularly introduced to Pickle Barrel crowds was Chicago native Mark Fenske. Influenced by Tom Dreesen and Jim Wiggins, among others, Fenske continued to perform stand-up before moving to California, where he appeared in the television shows *Happy Days* and *Mork & Mindy*. In 1987, Fenske returned to Chicago and resumed his stand-up career. (Courtesy of Bill Brady; photograph by William Cramp.)

Long before Starbucks replaced neighborhood diners as a go-to place for java, a shared love of coffee led Larry (above) and Jim (right) McManus to the Maroon Raccoon in Rosemont, where serendipity struck, and the brothers found their next comedy showroom. Like other McManus brothers venues, which the brothers viewed as places that offered an informal education for comedians, the place was called the Comedy College, and it became Chicago's first full-time comedy club. After Ed Hellenbrand assumed control, the McManus brothers continued to book comedy shows elsewhere, including at the Stable Restaurant and Lounge in Harwood Heights. In 1986, Larry opened the short-lived Chicago Comedyland club in the back room of a bar on Lincoln Avenue. Larry passed away in 2009; he also worked as a hypnotherapist for more than 30 years. (Both, courtesy of Susan Garstki McManus.)

Oak Park native Judy Tenuta first took the stage at the original Kingston Mines in Chicago. Named Best Female Comedy Club Stand-Up Comic at the 1988 American Comedy Awards, Tenuta has also received two Grammy nominations for her comedy albums and has starred in stand-up specials on HBO and Showtime. (Courtesy of Bill Brady.)

Tired of the theater scene, Brad Wethern turned to stand-up in 1975, appearing at Punchinello's and Ratso's, where he became a regular after the emcee for a variety show failed to attend. Wethern also worked at the Playboy Club in Chicago. As of 2014, Wethern was working as a realtor in California. (Courtesy of Brad Wethern.)

It was not unusual for Chicago comedians who performed at Comedy College shows to join Larry and Jim McManus for publicity pictures staged in odd places. Pictured here in the early morning hours at Chicago's O'Hare Airport are, from left to right, Judy Tenuta, Bob Rumba, Brad Wethern, Larry McManus, and Jim McManus. (Courtesy of Susan Garstki McManus.)

After his comedy team disbanded, Bob Rumba turned to ventriloquism and was never wanting for a stage partner, as he surrounded himself with a variety of characters, including Darby (left) and Dabney. As a look-alike, Rumba has worked in Branson, Missouri, and appeared in national television and print advertisements, frequently suiting up as Charlie Chaplin or Groucho Marx. (Courtesy of Bob Rumba; photograph by William Cramp.)

After Larry and Jim McManus parted ways with "Big" Ed Hellenbrand (left), the Comedy College became the Comedy Cottage when Hellenbrand placed black tape across the two Ls in "College" and left the misspelled word on the sign for almost a year. As a club owner, Hellenbrand ran hot and cold with comedians, although many comics fondly recall a night after a show when they were playing basketball on a rusty rim in the parking lot and Big Ed emerged from the club, grabbed the ball, and said, "All right, let's pick teams." Hellenbrand is pictured above with ventriloquist Bob Rumba, who had a "Little Ed" dummy made and used it at the club to the delight of audiences. Because the crowds at Comedy Cottage left little room for comics to hang out before taking the stage, Hellenbrand often complained about comics standing in the aisles, a habit reflected in his written comment on this photograph. Hellenbrand passed away in 2008. (Courtesy of Bob Rumba.)

After performing stand-up for many years, with much of his material a reflection of his partying lifestyle, Chicago native Jeff Allen began changing his act and life in the mid-1980s. He has since become one of the top Christian stand-up comics in the country and has starred in Comedy Central, Showtime, and VH1 specials and was a featured performer at Pres. George W. Bush's inauguration. (Courtesy of Bill Brady; photograph by William Cramp.)

Doing crowd work between sets and two years of studying influential comics like Jerry Dye and Ed Fiala helped convince singer Nick Cosentino to quit working as a musician and try stand-up at the Comedy Cottage. Soon, New York and Las Vegas called, and the Chicago native opened for Frankie Valli and David Copperfield. (Courtesy of Bill Brady; photograph by Denny Weber.)

A stand-up since 1982, when he took the stage at the Comedy Cottage, Greg Glienna wrote, directed, and starred in the original version of *Meet the Parents*, which was funded by Emo Philips. Universal Pictures bought the rights to the script and remade it as the 2000 movie starring Ben Stiller and Robert De Niro. Glienna also wrote *A Guy Thing* and directed *Relative Strangers*. (Courtesy of Bill Brady.)

Teddy LeRoi was a comedian other comics stayed to watch. In a 1982 article, *Chicago Tribune* reviewer Larry Kart wrote that the 21-year-old LeRoi flashed touches of Bill Cosby and Richard Pryor, and that while LeRoi might be compared to Eddie Murphy, "potentially he's much better than that." Sadly, LeRoi passed away in the early 1990s. (Courtesy of Bill Brady; photograph by Denny Weber.)

George Carlin was known to stop by the Comedy Cottage, as he was very familiar with the city. In the early 1960s, the comedy legend lived in Chicago, where he got paid to work at the Playboy Club and performed "free sets at the Rising Moon and Earl of Old Town." Carlin also spent some of his "free time with the folksies, rock 'n' rollers, [and] people from Second City," according to his autobiography, *Last Words*. (Courtesy of Denise Mix.)

Although Chicago native Vince Maranto passed on the chance to see George Carlin perform at Summerfest in Milwaukee in 1972—a show at which Carlin was arrested for obscenity moments after he stepped off the stage after completing his set—the experience proved to be a conversation starter when Maranto met Carlin years later. A stand-up since 1982, Maranto has appeared on numerous local and national television shows. (Courtesy of Vince Maranto.)

Raised in the northwest suburbs of Chicago, Tim Harrison was among the second wave of comics to go through the Comedy Cottage. Harrison started his career in 1982 and received needed direction from Vince Maranto. Harrison toured the country as a headliner, eventually booking a main stage performance at the Sahara Hotel in Las Vegas. (Courtesy of Bill Brady.)

Comedian Carl LaBove's interest in Michael Alexander's leather jacket led LaBove to pull the vacationing Alexander (pictured) out of line at the Comedy Store in Los Angeles and invite him backstage. While observing from the wings, Alexander became hooked on stand-up and, upon returning home to Chicago, began performing at the Cottage. He later worked as a staff writer for *The Arsenio Hall Show*. (Courtesy of Bill Brady.)

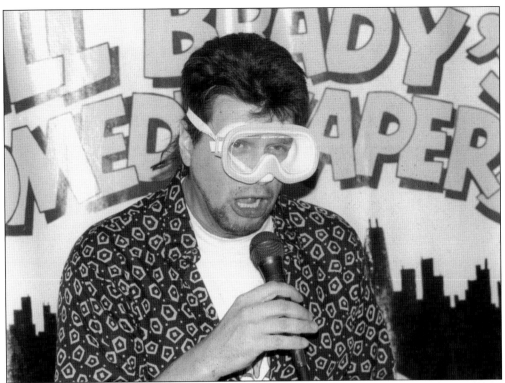

An impressionist whose send-ups of Harry Caray, Ozzy Osbourne, and Sylvester Stallone never failed to amuse crowds, Bob Jay first performed at Sally's Stage, a vaudeville-esque pizza parlor in Chicago, and then at the Cottage. In addition to doing comedy, Jay also works as a voice actor. (Courtesy of Bill Brady; photograph by Denny Weber.)

Graduates of the Players Workshop at Second City, Duck Logic thrived in comedy clubs and produced the *Duck Logic Comedy Cavalcade*, a weekly comedy program on Chicago radio station WLUP-AM. In recent years, their humor has appeared exclusively on their self-titled website. Duck Logic members are, from left to right, Dave-id Dunlosky, Michael Crawford, Tim Thomas, James F. Russell, and Walter Michka. (Courtesy of Duck Logic.)

A stand-up for more than 30 years, John Fox performed on *The Tonight Show* several times as well as *Opening Night at Rodney's Place*, Rodney Dangerfield's 1989 HBO special. The Zion native was the subject of many John Belushi–like tales—some true, some fabricated. Before succumbing to colon cancer in 2012, Fox established the John Fox Memorial Fund to help fund cancer screenings for comedians without health insurance. (Courtesy of Zanies.)

Today, high-rise office buildings and hotels occupy much of the land along North River Road where the Comedy Cottage once stood. (Photograph by Vince Vieceli.)

Two

THE COMEDY WOMB

In the mid-1970s, Mangam's Chateau, the longtime nightclub in its waning days, was located at the east end of Ogden Avenue in Lyons, and the west end of the avenue contained strip clubs and rock bars.

When comedian Jerry Dye agreed to meet a buddy for a drink in the west end, they retreated to a bar above the nearby Pines Restaurant. As Dye glanced around the place—a bar with hundreds of pennies affixed to the bar top—he thought, "How could this dump not be a comedy club?" Knowing upcoming Playboy Club gigs would keep him occupied, Dye relayed his idea to fellow comedians Ed Fiala, Ted Holum, and Ken Smith, who approached the space's owner, Nate Passaro.

"Nate was an old hypnotist, and he said as long as he could come up once or twice and do a show, we could give [comedy] a try," Holum said. Naturally, the comics agreed.

For a club name, comedian Jim Wiggins's wife, Joan, suggested the Comedy Womb—an apt name for a place "Where Comedians Are Born." In 1976, Fiala, Holum, and Smith made the club and slogan official when they began showcasing stand-up comedy twice per night Wednesday through Saturday. The place was a hit.

"We used to have people waiting [outside] for, like, an hour to get into the second show," said Chrissie Frey, an early Womb manager and one of the few women in a predominately male environment. "At the time, there were few girls [performing stand-up]," Frey said. "Just Judy [Tenuta] and Diane Lambert. I can't remember another girl."

Though there was not a drink minimum, patrons paid a $2 cover charge that went toward compensating the comedians—a Chicago first—with the average pay for comedians ranging between $2 and $3 per show. The policy forced Comedy Cottage owner Ed Hellenbrand's hand, and he began paying talent, too. In turn, comedians eagerly made the 40-mile round trip between the Cottage and Womb to perform in as many as four shows per night.

In the late 1970s, landlord woes forced the Womb to move across the street for a short period before it reverted to its original location. Womb ownership changed hands over the following years before the place finally closed in 1996.

Ted Holum performed with Ed Fiala on *The Tonight Show* when Steve Allen was the guest host on March 7, 1982. Just the week before, Allen had watched the pair bring the laughs at a Chicago benefit. As both Holum and Fiala grew more confident, they split up and embarked on successful solo careers. Holum was instrumental in opening the Comedy Womb and Who's on 1st. (Courtesy of Bill Brady; photograph by William Cramp.)

Located on Ogden Avenue in Lyons, Illinois, the Comedy Womb occupied the upstairs part of Sherwood Castle, which later became the Pines Restaurant. Initially, crowds never passed through the downstairs area, only entering the Womb through this outside stairwell on the east side of the building. (Courtesy of Bill Brady.)

A founder of the Comedy Womb, Ed Fiala made his *Tonight Show* debut on March 7, 1982, with comedy partner Ted Holum. Fiala compiled a book of neologisms entitled *Everyday Man's Dictionary*, which he used in his act. Fiala's strength was sound effects, as he mimicked winter blizzards, motorbikes, power tools, and more. Fiala passed away in 2002. (Courtesy of Bill Brady.)

The building on Ogden Avenue that housed the Womb was demolished in the late 1990s to make room for condominiums, with this unit built in the former location of the Womb's parking lot. This 2013 photograph was taken across the street from where the Womb was located. (Photograph by Vince Vieceli.)

After getting his start at Chicago's first full-time comedy club, the Comedy Cottage, Jerry Dye was instrumental in opening the second when the tacky bar that he thought might work as a comedy club became the Comedy Womb. It lasted for 20 years. (Courtesy of Chrissie Frey.)

For a short stint in 1978, the Comedy Womb moved to a vacant room across the street from Sherwood Castle. Such moves often hurt businesses, but because stand-up comedy itself was a hot commodity in the late 1970s, people still packed the new Womb. (Courtesy of Chrissie Frey.)

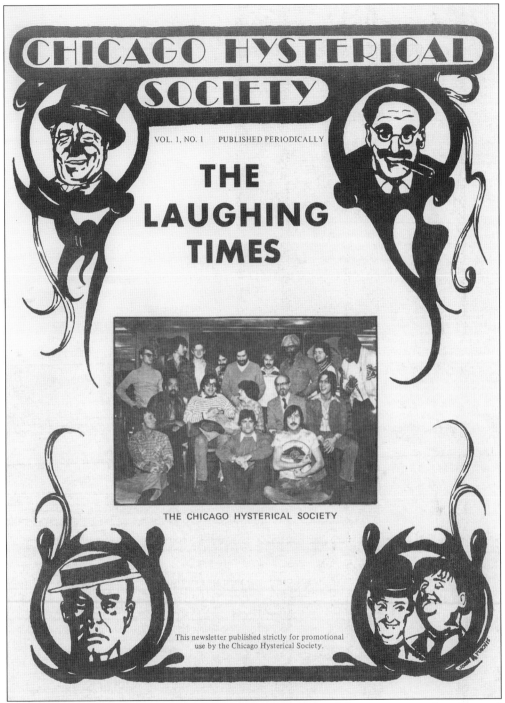

CHICAGO HYSTERICAL SOCIETY

VOL. 1, NO. 1   PUBLISHED PERIODICALLY

THE LAUGHING TIMES

THE CHICAGO HYSTERICAL SOCIETY

This newsletter published strictly for promotional use by the Chicago Hysterical Society.

Organized by Ted Holum and Ed Fiala, the Chicago Hysterical Society promoted professional comedy in Chicago and assisted the development of performers. The group published a monthly newsletter that, in 1978, also noted the various celebrities who visited the Womb or the Comedy Cottage, including Jerry Van Dyke, Bert Convy, Jay Leno, Canadian comedian Mike Neun, and members of the Doobie Brothers. (Courtesy of Bill Brady.)

The Comedy Womb logo incorporated Charlie Chaplin. Pictured here are, from left to right, (first row) Deb Zajac and Sunee Jentry; (second row) unidentified, Paul Barnes, Mark Shufeldt, and unidentified. Shufeldt attended the Womb's opening night and recalls the place being "packed to the gills." From 1976 to 1996, he worked as doorman, manager, booker, and, later, co-owner. (Courtesy of the William Cramp estate; photograph by William Cramp.)

Joe Conti was not the only comedy veteran who recognized that new fans could be won over at a comedy club. Leonard Barr, also known as Dean Martin's uncle, performed at the Womb shortly before his death in 1980. (Courtesy of Bill Brady.)

A regular at Zanies Comedy Club, Larry Reeb first learned his craft at the Comedy Womb (where Reeb is performing in the photograph at right) and the Comedy Cottage. The Dwight, Illinois, native has appeared on VH1's *Stand-Up Spotlight* and in the HBO special *Opening Night at Rodney's Place*, hosted by Rodney Dangerfield. (Courtesy of Chrissie Frey.)

Primarily a stand-up when he stopped by the Womb in the late 1970s, the Austrian-born Bill Kirchenbauer became a familiar face to audiences thereafter, appearing as a regular or guest star on numerous television shows, including *Growing Pains* and *Just the Ten of Us*. (Courtesy of Bill Brady.)

"Site-specific extrovert" is how Chicago native Danny Storts explains his stage work despite being something of an introvert. Seeing his friend Brad Wethern perform stand-up during the late 1970s enticed Storts to follow suit, which started a long career that has seen him open for Elvis Costello, Stephen Stills, and Chicago. (Courtesy of Chrissie Frey.)

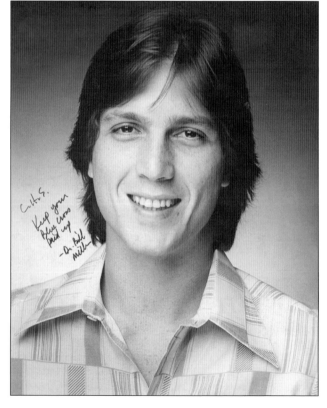

Yes, Dr. Bill Miller is a bona fide physician. After growing up in Los Angeles and graduating from University of California, Los Angeles, Miller began performing at comedy clubs while in med school at Northwestern University. After taking a 15-year hiatus to raise his children, Miller returned to clubs to perform his one-man show, *Doctors Are People Too*. (Courtesy of Chrissie Frey.)

Audiences continued to laugh at crowd favorite Carla Filisha's work after she left the stand-up circuit, even if they did not know it. In the early 1990s, the Riverside native moved to Hollywood, where she has written for several television shows, including *Still Standing* and *Mike and Molly*. (Courtesy of Zanies.)

Audiences also are more familiar with Joey Gutierrez's offstage work, as the Calumet City native wrote many of the opening monologues on *Seinfeld*. In 2002, Gutierrez and longtime partner Diane Burroughs created the television sitcom *Still Standing*. Burroughs, a Mount Prospect native, is also a former comic. (Courtesy of the William Cramp estate; photograph by William Cramp.)

Mount Greenwood native Margaret Smith began her stand-up career locally in the early 1980s, and in 1995, she won the American Comedy Award for Funniest Female Stand-Up Comic. Smith won six Daytime Emmy Awards as a writer and producer for *The Ellen DeGeneres Show*. (Courtesy of Zanies.)

Naperville native Bob Odenkirk performed stand-up and improv comedy in Chicago before joining *Saturday Night Live* as a writer. In the 1990s, he teamed with David Cross to create and star in the HBO sketch comedy series *Mr. Show with Bob and David*, which became a cult favorite. In 2009, Odenkirk landed his breakthrough role of Saul Goodman in *Breaking Bad*. (Courtesy of the William Cramp estate; photograph by William Cramp.)

After eyeing stand-up since childhood, A.J. Lentini began his career at the Comedy Womb in 1984 and later appeared on MTV's *Half-Hour Comedy Hour*. After moving west, the Joliet native embarked on a writing career and has written comedy material for *The Tonight Show with Jay Leno* and Wise Brother Media. (Courtesy of the William Cramp estate; photograph by William Cramp.)

Referencing the city's then-seedy image, Rick Ellis always joked that Lyons was the only place where even the police cars had "Girls Girls Girls" written on the side. Also a freelance writer, the Evansville, Indiana, native was the founder and managing editor of AllYourTV.com and AllYourScreens.com. (Courtesy of the William Cramp estate; photograph by William Cramp.)

Exceptionally honest but not crude enough to be overlooked for national television appearances, Brian Schmidt loved to focus on gender and once quipped, "You see a woman with a ton of makeup slapped on her face, and you wonder, if she washed it, will you see the numbers of where the colors are supposed to go?" (Courtesy of the William Cramp estate; photograph by William Cramp.)

Voted the Funniest Woman in Chicago at a 1990 contest at the Improv comedy club, Dea Staley was an ex-nurse and housewife who made the transition to the stage. Staley's husband and daughter were frequent topics in her act. (Courtesy of the William Cramp estate; photograph by William Cramp.)

For some comics, one-nighters served as the entry points of their careers. Influenced by Chicago comics Paul Kelly and Mike Toomey, Steger native Scot Wickmann started at the Apple Pub in Chicago in 1988 and later met his future wife at the Comedy Womb. Wickmann has opened for Paula Poundstone, Jeff Dunham, and Drew Carey. (Courtesy of Bill Brady.)

After beginning his comedy career in the early 1980s with the improv group Slippery When Wet, Mike Ostrowski switched to stand-up and has opened for Richard Lewis and Bill Burr, among others. Although Hollywood tempted him, Ostrowski remained in Chicago and worked for *Playboy Magazine* for 27 years. (Courtesy of the William Cramp estate; photograph by William Cramp.)

Influenced by Bill Cosby and Bob Newhart, Melrose Park native Pat Duax made his stand-up debut in 1978 at Kobart's Komedy Kove, one of Chicago's most short-lived clubs. (Courtesy of the William Cramp estate; photograph by William Cramp.)

Among comedians, Pat Duax was especially popular because when he was not performing, Duax (in truck) worked as a Good Humor ice cream man and often incorporated comedy clubs into his route. In line for ice cream are Bob Odenkirk (left), Comedy Womb faithful customer Dan McGrath (center), and an unidentified comic. (Courtesy of the William Cramp estate; photograph by William Cramp.)

Rickey Connor was a rare breed of stand-up, often leaving audiences short of breath at night and working as a respiratory therapist during the day. The Chicago native was also a Vietnam veteran and often performed on *Chicago Sun-Times* columnist Irv Kupcinet's Purple Heart Cruises on Lake Michigan. Connor passed away in 1999. (Courtesy of the William Cramp estate; photograph by William Cramp.)

An improv actor who made his stand-up debut at an open mic night at Sheffield's bar in 1987, Peter Moor was no more popular with audiences than when he did his routine about blues singers pointing out other blues singers coming through the front door. (Courtesy of the William Cramp estate; photograph by William Cramp.)

After stand-up, Kevin Lampe turned to politics and, in 1996, partnered with his wife Kitty Kurth to form Kurth Lampe, a Chicago-based strategic communications firm. As executive vice president, Lampe has worked during each presidential election cycle since 1988 and has served in variety of senior staff roles for presidential candidates. (Courtesy of the William Cramp estate; photograph by William Cramp.)

Known to comedy club audiences nationwide as "Jammin'" Kay Cammon, the talented comedienne is also an accomplished filmmaker and the host and producer of the 2010 documentary *Chicago: Comedy Womb to Comedy Boom.* (Courtesy of Bill Brady.)

Not only did Doug Doane perform at Chicago comedy clubs, the Elgin native opened some, too, including the Comedy Cellar in Lombard, the Schaumburg Comedy Club, and Roars in Highland Park. Working with Bert Borth, Doane also had a hand in opening the Funny Bone in Schaumburg. (Courtesy of Bill Brady; photograph by William Cramp.)

In June 2006, many believed that Chicago-born Joe Restivo (pictured in the 1970s), had passed away when news spread that a Los Angeles comedian with the same name had died. Oddly, "Chicago" Joe Restivo then died in December 2007. The Los Angeles Joe Restivo was the former co-owner of Vitello's restaurant, where actor Robert Blake and his wife dined the night she was murdered. (Courtesy of Chrissie Frey.)

For Chicago native John Midas, his act centered around his life experiences, including the time he got strip-searched after being pulled over for a speeding violation on the Ohio Turnpike. In 1985, Midas opened for Jay Leno and received high praise from the future *Tonight Show* host. Midas started his comedy career in 1979. (Courtesy of Zanies.)

In 1986, veteran comedian John Tambirino won the First Annual Bob Collins Comedy Bowl, named after the popular WGN radio morning man. In recapping the contest, the *Chicago Tribune* reported that the panel of judges featured two newspaper columnists, a political satirist, a television critic, and "for some strange reason, a beer company executive." (Courtesy of the William Cramp estate; photograph by William Cramp.)

It was not so much Morey Amsterdam as it was the fun that Amsterdam was having on *The Dick Van Dyke Show* that steered Westchester's Vince Vieceli into comedy. A bigger push came in the late 1980s when Dennis Miller used material that Vieceli had submitted for a "Weekend Update" segment on *Saturday Night Live*. For Vieceli, this book was a labor of love. (Courtesy of Vince Vieceli.)

When his job required a move to Florida in 1990, Chicagoan Will Shore took his wife Janet's suggestion and filled the time he normally spent with friends and family by trying comedy at a Daytona Beach club. In Chicago, Shore was one of the last owners of the Comedy Womb, and after leaving comedy, he became a minister. (Courtesy of Bill Brady.)

An unpredictable performer who brought his own applause sign, Ira Novos played keyboards and sometimes ended his act with a little tune on the stump fiddle. (Courtesy of the William Cramp estate; photograph by William Cramp.)

If the Comedy Womb itself had a fault, it was the limited space at the back of the room, where comics liked to hang out or quietly go over their jokes. Here, the tiny hallway between the restrooms provides refuge for comedians Ken Swann (left) and Bill Hutson. Swann passed away in 2008. (Courtesy of the William Cramp estate; photograph by William Cramp.)

At the Comedy Womb, "Where Comedians Are Born," sometimes conception was as simple as pointing a camera at the comics. Above, Rich Purpura (left) and Mark Roberts ham it up. Below, Pat Duax (left) surprises Rickey Connor. (Both courtesy of the William Cramp estate; photographs by William Cramp.)

Though the group's goals were formidable, the Chicago Hysterical Society folded after a few years. Pictured here are, from left to right, (first row) Jerry Dye, unidentified, and Ted Holum; (second row) Orlando Reyes, Tony Papaleo, unidentified, Norman Temple, and Dr. Bill Miller; (third row); unidentified, Emo Philips, Jeff Michalski, Ed Fiala, Paul Kelly, Frank Hooper, James Wesley Jackson, Jim Fay, and Reggie Sykes. (Courtesy of Frank Hooper.)

In 2011, former Comedy Womb employees and three generations of comedians gathered for the 35th anniversary of the Comedy Womb's opening. Because of tour schedules and changes in residences, some attendees had not seen one another in decades. Jerry Dye, Chrissie Frey, and Deb Zajac organized the event. (Courtesy of Ginger Frey Nicolaou.)

Three

BILL BRADY'S COMEDY CAPERS AT THE BARREL OF LAUGHS

With the arrival of full-time clubs, comedians began referring to gigs that gave them stage time one night per week as "one-nighters." Even today, one-nighters provide comics with extra stage time and cash, and while most one-night shows failed to expand beyond that limited engagement, one Chicago gig not only beat the odds, but went on to make regional history, too.

Bill Brady's Comedy Capers, named for the comic who booked and hosted the shows, consisted of several one-nighters staged primarily in the southern and western suburbs of Chicago, including Slips in Dalton on Wednesdays, Groucho's Bar and Grill in Chicago on Thursdays, and Lorenzo's in Riverdale on Fridays. Later, other stops on the circuit featured Senese's Vineyard in Darien and Puttin' on the Ritz in Lombard. Still, no matter the week, Bill Brady's Comedy Capers always began on Tuesdays at Senese's Winery Restaurant and Lounge in Oak Lawn, with the first show held in 1977. The opening night comedians included Jerry Dye, Paul Kelly, James Wesley Jackson, Diane Lambert, Emo Phillips, and Judy Tenuta.

As the crowds got larger, Senese's owners, Tom and Terry Senese, added a second night of comedy on Wednesdays before moving away from the dance music and DJs of the late 1970s and converting the lounge into Chicago's third full-time comedy club. Unveiled in 1983, Senese's Barrel of Laughs Comedy Club, the "Home of Bill Brady's Comedy Capers," offered as many as nine shows per week and took its name from a large wooden barrel that served as canopy around the lounge's southern door. To demonstrate that the restaurant and new comedy club were still a joint venture, Senese's began offering a dinner/show package; it was an "under one roof" sales pitch that few other clubs could offer. Another difference at the Barrel of Laughs was the language, as comedians were prohibited from using the "f-word."

But like Chicago's other original comedy clubs, the Barrel of Laughs ran its course and eventually closed in 2010. With 33 years of shows, Bill Brady's Comedy Capers was the longest-running comedy show in the Midwest.

Senese's used wine barrels as part of its decor throughout the restaurant and lounge. Patrons entered through this barrel-shaped front door, so it was only natural to name the comedy club "Barrel of Laughs." The club's logo was a barrel surrounded by three laughing figures. (Courtesy of Bill Brady; photograph by Denny Weber.)

Who changes a sign in a tuxedo? The answer: Bill Brady. Known for his sharp dress sense, Brady is pictured adjusting the sign for his fifth-anniversary show; Brady would celebrate 28 more anniversaries at the club. (Courtesy of Bill Brady; photograph by William Cramp.)

Host of Bill Brady's Comedy Capers at the Barrel of Laughs, Brady has also performed at other comedy clubs around the country and on cruise ships. The veteran comedian has performed on *The Oprah Winfrey Show*, hosted the cable television program *Chicago at Large*, and appeared as an extra in *Prison Break* and the movie *Tapioca*, which stars Ben Vereen and Mike Houlihan. (Courtesy of Bill Brady.)

After meeting Tom Senese (left) while working as a union business agent in 1972, Bill Brady began deejaying at a bar owned by Tom's brother, Dick, in 1974. Ironically, two waitresses visiting from the Womb encouraged Brady to try stand-up, which ultimately led to the opening of the Barrel of Laughs and a lifelong friendship between Brady and the Seneses. (Courtesy of Bill Brady.)

Judy Tenuta, also known as "the Love Goddess," charmed the audience with her accordion and wisecracks at the first Comedy Capers show at Senese's. (Courtesy of Bill Brady; photograph by William Cramp.)

Originally from Greenwood, Mississippi, James Wesley Jackson moved to Chicago just in time for Senese's first night of comedy, which is pictured below. Jackson, who dubs himself an "environmedian," since his humor stems from the environment around him, was the longtime opening act for Parliament-Funkadelic. (Courtesy of Bill Brady.)

A stand-up since 1976, Downers Grove native Emo Philips has performed more than 6,000 comedy shows, including opening night at Senese's. Philips was cited by Jay Leno as the "best joke writer in America," and three of Philips's jokes made GQ magazine's June 1999 list of the Top 75 Jokes of All Time, as voted on by comedians. Philips has released three comedy albums. (Courtesy of the William Cramp estate; photograph by William Cramp.)

James Wesley Jackson is surrounded by moustaches as Ted Holum (left) and Ed Fiala (right) smile at the end of a performance at the "Barrel." (Courtesy of Bill Brady.)

53

An old-school comic who danced, sang, and did impressions, Joe Conti performed for several decades at Mangam's Chateau, doing whatever it took to entertain the audience. Conti also recorded his first album, *Live at Mangam's Chateau*, at the nightclub. During his career, which began in 1936, Conti (as a child) appeared in movies with Alan Ladd and John Garfield. Conti passed away in 1997. (Courtesy of Bill Brady; photograph by Denny Weber.)

Jim Wiggins (left) and Joe Conti are pictured here as a couple of old buddies sitting around and talking about the good ol' days. (Courtesy of Bill Brady.)

Originally from Mississippi, Jerry Dye was one of the founders of the Comedy Womb, and following a move to Los Angeles, he became a regular on *The Big Show* and a contributing writer for the Redd Foxx sitcom *Sanford and Son*. Dye has opened for some of the Blue Collar Comedy comedians and appeared with Ron White on Truckstop Comedy albums. (Courtesy of Bill Brady; photograph by William Cramp.)

While many Chicago comedians left town (and stand-up comedy in general) for Hollywood, Paul Kelly remained true to his stand-up roots, headlining clubs throughout the United States and Canada after starting to do comedy in 1975. Representing the Barrel of Laughs, Kelly won the first WGN Comedy Bowl contest, and he has appeared on *An Evening at the Improv* and *Comedy on the Road*, among other shows. (Courtesy of Bill Brady; photograph by William Cramp.)

Anniversary shows at the Barrel of Laughs were often highlighted by performances from comedians who had previously worked the club. Pictured here are, from left to right, (first row) Paul Kelly, Jimmy Pardo, and Pete Schwaba; (second row) Steve Seagren, Tim Cavanagh, and Mike Toomey; (third row, standing) Emo Philips and Bill Brady. (Courtesy of Bill Brady.)

Impressionists say that getting someone's voice down is one thing, but putting that same person in a new and different situation is another. Frank Hooper began his comedy career in 1976 and quickly demonstrated his uncanny ability to do the latter; however, given the uncertainty of the entertainment business, Hooper pursued other interests. (Courtesy of Bill Brady; photograph by William Cramp.)

Chicago native John Caponera first began appearing at the Barrel of Laughs in 1979, performing impressions of old-time baseball players that turned into play-by-play recaps of the "game." Years later, Caponera starred in the sitcom *The Good Life* with Drew Carey. (Courtesy of Bill Brady; photograph by William Cramp.)

Originally a magician who performed on Chicago's South Side, Rich Purpura began adding more comedy to his act and, in turn, allowing the tricks to become more outrageous over time. The change made his career, as Purpura has now worked for Disney Cruise Line for more than 15 years. (Courtesy of Bill Brady; photograph by William Cramp.)

Chicago's own Steve Rudnick (right) and Leo Benvenuti toured and worked the Playboy Club in Lake Geneva, where they once met and received praise from Lenny Bruce's mother. The comedy team—Steve & Leo—became well known as screenwriters; they penned *Kicking & Screaming*, which starred the Chicago Bears' Mike Ditka; *Space Jam*, featuring Chicago icons Bill Murray and Michael Jordan; and *The Santa Clause*. (Courtesy of Bill Brady.)

Though his brand of humor was considered blue by some, Orlando Reyes was a master at working the crowd and cooking soul food—two talents that he often displayed at comedy clubs, where he would hold cooking demonstrations during or after performances. In the 1990s, Reyes became a co-owner of the Comedy Womb. Reyes passed away in 2006. (Courtesy of Bill Brady.)

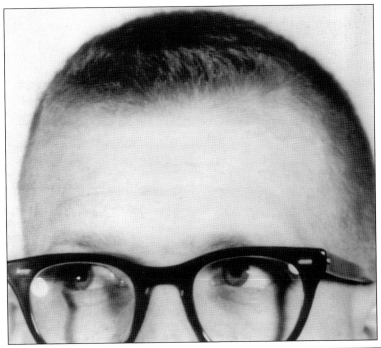

Chicago's comedy-hungry audiences attracted outside talent like Cleveland native Drew Carey, who performed at the Barrel of Laughs in 1987. Appearances on *The Tonight Show* and *Late Night With David Letterman* helped Carey land his own sitcom, *The Drew Carey Show*. John Caponera appeared in at least one episode of the show. (Courtesy of Bill Brady.)

A magician since age 17, Bill Malone began performing at Little Bit O' Magic on Chicago's South Side before branching out into comedy clubs like the Barrel. Following a move to Florida, Malone worked resorts, made numerous television appearances, and—with the Boca Resort Hotel and Club—opened Malone's Magic Bar, which he operated from 1995 through 2005. Malone is a previous winner of the International Magicians Society's Merlin Award. (Courtesy of Bill Brady.)

Elmhurst's own Steve Seagren first began performing stand-up at Who's on 1st in 1983 and was the only person to hit Bill Brady with a pie in the face while Brady was on stage. As an actor, Seagren has appeared in *How I Met Your Mother*, *My Name is Earl*, and *Everybody Hates Chris*, which was cocreated by Chicago native Ali LeRoi. (Courtesy of Bill Brady; photograph by Denny Weber.)

Diane Alaimo was a late bloomer who began her comedy career at the age of 30 before quitting her day job in 1990 to follow her passion and work full-time as a comedian. Italian family life was the focus of much of Alaimo's act, and she appeared on Showtime, the Comedy Channel Network, HBO, MTV, and BET. Loved by all, Alaimo passed away in 2001. (Courtesy of Bill Brady; photograph by Denny Weber.)

Raised in Tolono, Illinois, Mark Roberts performed stand-up in Chicago before moving to Hollywood, where he appeared on *The Tonight Show* seven times. It was Roberts' playwriting that caught the attention of television producer Chuck Lorre, who hired Roberts to write for *Two and a Half Men*. Roberts went on to create the sitcom *Mike and Molly*, which stars Plainfield, Illinois, native Melissa McCarthy. (Courtesy of Bill Brady.)

Bill Leff, an improv performer and stand-up in the mid-1980s, saw his career expand at the end of the decade with appearances in the movies *Major League* and *Major League II*. Shortly thereafter, Leff's appearance as a guest on Wendy Snyder's radio show led to the pair working as a team for several Chicago radio stations, including WLUP, WKQX, WLS, and WGN. (Courtesy of Bill Brady; photograph by Denny Weber.)

A hulky, intimidating presence when he stepped onto the stage, Harry Hickstein had audiences wondering if he was not a comic but rather a mob enforcer or a member of the Hell's Angels. Actually, Hickstein, also known as "Mister Big Stuff," was quite the giant teddy bear—and a funny one, at that. Hickstein, who is also an actor, appeared in *An Innocent Man*. (Courtesy of Bill Brady; photograph by Denny Weber.)

With his performances that felt more the telling of a life story (but funnier), Jim Higgins was a highly sought comedian during the 1980s and 1990s. (Courtesy of Bill Brady; photograph by Denny Weber.)

William "Bill" Cramp (left) was not just a photographer; he was also a willing participant when a performer needed one. Here, Cramp lends a hand to magician Dr. Nick Rizzo. As a club photographer, Cramp captured many Chicago comedians on film as well as taking their headshots. Without his dedication, this book would not be possible (or as endearing). (Courtesy of Bill Brady.)

From left to right, Bill Brady, Jim Wiggins, Jerry Dye, and Paul Kelly reminisce about so many years, so many shows, and so much talent as they listen to the "new kids" at the Barrel of Laughs. (Courtesy of Bill Brady.)

Not all Chicago comedians hit the small screen via Hollywood. Mike Toomey did it in his hometown, becoming a full-time member of the *WGN Morning News* team in 2013 after previously contributing to the program as himself or as satirical sportscaster Skip Parker. In addition to doing stand-up and television, Toomey also created and starred in his own one-man comedy show, *TV & Me*. (Courtesy of Bill Brady; photograph by Denny Weber.)

As funny as the comedian is and as receptive as the crowds are, sometimes the promise of steadier work and better pay persuades budding comics to withdraw from the craft and pursue another line of work. Jeff Schlesinger falls into that category. The former comic now works as a lawyer. He is the father of singer Kiely Schlesinger. (Courtesy of Bill Brady; photograph by William Cramp.)

Raised in Bensenville (near Chicago O'Hare International Airport's number four runway, to be exact), Rich Brown toured the Midwest and opened for Jerry Seinfeld before moving to Hollywood. Brown worked as a "punch-up" writer for several Farrelly brothers' films, including *Me, Myself and Irene*; *Shallow Hal*; and *Dumb and Dumber To*. (Courtesy of Bill Brady; photograph by Denny Weber.)

A product of Chicago's southwest side, Jimmy Dore cut his teeth in Chicago's comedy clubs before moving west. Dore starred in several Comedy Central specials and has appeared on *Jimmy Kimmel Live*, *Last Comic Standing*, and *The Late Late Show with Craig Ferguson*. A writer and performer in the off-Broadway hit *The Marijuana-Logues*, Dore also hosts a weekly radio show in Los Angeles. (Courtesy of Zanies.)

Among the sharpest Chicago comics, Dwayne Kennedy was summed up best by the *Chicago Tribune*'s Allan Johnson, who wrote, "[Kennedy] displays a deft talent for social commentary as he jabs racism, the hip-hop culture, and gangs." A Jury Award winner for Best Stand-Up at the 2002 US Comedy Arts Festival, Kennedy has appeared on *Late Show with David Letterman* and *Late Night with Conan O'Brien*. (Courtesy of Bill Brady; photograph by Denny Weber.)

Chicago native Gerry Grossman is one part comedian and one part guitarist, a reflection of his many years spent on the road as a musician in the 1960s and 1970s. Grossman has played with the Byrds, Cheap Trick, and REO Speedwagon, among others. Grossman is known as the "Human Jukebox," as he challenges audiences to name old rock 'n' roll songs that he cannot play. (Courtesy of Bill Brady; photograph by Denny Weber.)

A former interstate truck driver and Golden Gloves boxer (he won six times in six bouts), Brooklyn's Rocky LaPorte had been performing stand-up in Chicago for just two years when he placed second in the 1989 WGN Comedy Bowl competition. Since then, LaPorte has appeared on *The Tonight Show* and *An Evening at the Improv* and starred in his own sitcom pilot for CBS. (Courtesy of Bill Brady; photograph by Denny Weber.)

Veteran comedian Tim Walkoe has performed at more than 100 clubs nationwide, including the Comedy Stop in Las Vegas and the Comedy Store in Los Angeles. He also played Mayor Emerson Bowden in the 2001 television show *Murder in Small Town X*. (Courtesy of Bill Brady; photograph by Denny Weber.)

The 2013 winner of the Diamond Jo Casino's Comedy $10K contest, held in Dubuque, Iowa, Tinley Parks native Brian Hicks first began performing comedy at Riddles Comedy Club in 1999 and is among many comics upholding Chicago's reputation for producing strong stand-ups. (Courtesy of Bill Brady.)

A comedian since the late 1990s, Fritz Nothnagel has made a name for himself in Chicago using a dry, deadpan approach that reminds many of Bob Newhart. (Courtesy of Bill Brady.)

Brian Noonan, a veteran touring comedian who has appeared on *The Tonight Show with Jay Leno*, later made the leap to television actor, appearing in *Malcolm in the Middle*, *It's All Relative*, and *In-Laws* before returning to Chicago and landing a job as an overnight host on WGN Radio. (Courtesy of Bill Brady; photograph by William Cramp.)

Unlike most comedians, Dale Irvin is also a certified professional speaker, as dubbed by the National Speakers Association; he is one of only 190 speakers in the world to hold this honor. (Courtesy of Bill Brady.)

The passing of loved ones often prompts family members to embark on long, put-off goals, and Chicago native Bill Gorgo is no different. After his father died in the early 1980s, Gorgo began doing stand-up, performing at Larry McManus's Comedyland before his second passion won out and he became a high school teacher in Chicago. He continued doing stand-up for stress relief. (Courtesy of Bill Gorgo.)

A product of Chicago's Beverly neighborhood, Pat McGreal used the talent he nurtured in local clubs and the contacts he made to establish a comedy-writing career, including a stint with *The Rosie O'Donnell Show*. In 2013, the *Chicago Tribune* began running *Future Shock*, a comic created by Pat and his brother Jim, in the newspaper every Sunday. (Courtesy of Bill Brady; photograph by Denny Weber.)

Four

ZANIES COMEDY CLUB

Strangely, Chicago's oldest original comedy club is one that has endured competition from a nearby comedy institution. Located on Wells Street, Zanies Comedy Club is just a few storefronts south of the Second City theater, and while competition between the two is not quite direct—Zanies offers stand-up while Second City is known for sketch and improv comedy—the fact that Zanies has endured for more than 35 years is a testament to its staying power.

Opened in Chicago's Old Town neighborhood in 1978 by three budding entrepreneurs, Zanies, Chicago's fourth full-time comedy club, was inspired by the Domino Lounge on Walton Street, a place the *Chicago Tribune* described as "a tiny conventioneers' hangout where Frank Penning packs them in with his mixture of insults and dirty jokes." At Zanies, the comedy was much cleaner. In fact, for several years, the club was home to *Byrne Baby Byrne*, a political satire named for Chicago's then-mayor Jane Byrne.

But with stand-up still in its infancy, Zanies' original owners soon experienced financial woes, and just two years after the club opened, it was taken over by the building's landlord, Rick Uchwat. Uchwat—a Vietnam veteran who spent three months in a full-body cast after the jeep he was riding in was either shelled or hit a mine—was no stranger to challenges. Still, none of Uchwat's other Chicago nightclubs were like Zanies.

"Rick wasn't sure he wanted to keep [Zanies] open," said Bert Haas, current executive vice president of Zanies.

After deciding to give it a go, Uchwat kept the Zanies name but made several changes that not only became the club's trademarks but also lasted for decades. Among Uchwat's first moves was promoting Haas, who had been hired as a waiter by the previous regime, to floor manager. Over the following 30 years, Uchwat and Haas expanded the business, opening locations in Nashville, Tennessee, and then locally in St. Charles, Mount Prospect, Vernon Hills, and Rosemont. Today, only the Chicago, St. Charles, and Rosemont clubs remain open.

Uchwat succumbed to lung cancer in 2011. He was 64.

The crooked letters on the Zanies sign date back to the club's original owners and first sign, which had removable letters. As the owners got into some financial struggles, the sign-maintenance company erroneously repossessed the fixture before returning it separately from the letters. Believing "zany" should be reflected on the club's sign, Rick Uchwat swiveled the letters before putting the sign back up. (Photograph by Vince Vieceli.)

More than 350 comedians' headshots adorn the walls and ceiling beams at the Zanies on Wells Street. Audience members often take time to view the photographs before and after shows. (Photograph by Vince Vieceli.)

In addition to photographs, large portraits of comedians hang on the walls of every Zanies club. The idea was Rick Uchwat's, and the artwork is by Robert Fischer, who called his style "Bizzarte." The style swept the art world and prompted *People Magazine* to label Fischer the "Windy City Warhol." Fischer's art has been featured on *Late Night with David Letterman*, *The Oprah Winfrey Show*, and the *CBS Evening News*. In 1986, Fischer became the first artist from outside California to be featured at Spago restaurant. (Photograph by Vince Vieceli.)

Uchwat got the idea for the artwork, now considered a Zanies trademark, after seeing similar examples of it in the window of Fischer's studio, which was across the street from the club. The comedians whose portraits are on the walls include Jay Leno, Jerry Seinfeld, Richard Lewis, Emo Philips, John Caponera, and Larry Reeb. (Photograph by Vince Vieceli.)

Unsure what to do with Zanies when he assumed control in 1980, Rick Uchwat quickly took a liking to comedians and often tended bar at the club's Christmas party. Zanies executive vice president Bert Haas said, "Rick loved hanging out, so Zanies became an after hours place for all the comedians." (Courtesy of Zanies.)

Introduced to Chicago via Mister Kelly's, where the marquee once advertised him as "Jay L No" because the club did not have enough "e" tiles, Jay Leno (right) made regular stops at Zanies on Wells Street beginning in the early 1980s. Rick Uchwat is pictured with Leno. (Courtesy of Zanies.)

For comics, some nights it is better to forgo politeness and ask for stage time the Chicago way—just kidding! Back in the 1990s, former Chicago Bears tight end Tim Wrightman (right) tried his hand at stand-up and received direction from Tom Dreesen (left) and Zanies manager Bert Haas. (Courtesy of Zanies.)

Pictured with television icon Bozo the Clown, Bert Haas (left) began his Zanies career in February 1980 as a waiter. As Zanies expanded, so did Haas's role, and he eventually took the reins as executive vice president. Haas met his wife, comedian Sally Edwards (right), at Zanies. In 2013, they celebrated their 26th wedding anniversary. (Courtesy of Zanies.)

Author of *Comedy Mom! My Funny Stand-Up Life*, Sally Edwards made her stand-up debut at Zanies, where she met her future husband, Bert Haas. Years later, a pregnant Edwards was moments away from performing at the Who's on 1st comedy club when she went into early labor and had to be rushed to Elmhurst Hospital. Edwards and Haas have three children. (Courtesy of Bill Brady; photograph by William Cramp.)

In the 1980s, Jenny Jones toured the country as a stand-up comedian, so after she began taping her self-titled syndicated daytime talk show in Chicago, it was not unusual for Jones to drop by the city's comedy clubs. Here, Jones (second row, second from left) is pictured with Zanies staff members. (Courtesy of Zanies.)

In 1992, Jay Leno returned to Zanies to perform a benefit show for Chicago's unemployed. (Courtesy of Zanies.)

Recognized by *Chicago* magazine as one of the city's top comics, Larry Reeb, also known as "Uncle Lar," has been performing stand-up for more than 40 years, endlessly doling out tips and quips, like the night that a heckler yelled, "Talk about sex," to which Reeb replied, "Your parents shouldn't have had it." (Courtesy of Zanies.)

As many people have remarked, stand-up comedy was the rock n' roll of the 1980s, and it attracted performances from crossover artists like Steve Dahl and Garry Meier, a popular Chicago radio team. Pictured here are, from left to right, comedian Rich Hall, Dahl, Jay Leno, Rick Uchwat, and Meier. (Courtesy of Zanies.)

Danny Bonaduce was another Chicago personality who tried stand-up. Bonaduce costarred in the 1970s sitcom *The Partridge Family*. (Courtesy of Zanies.)

Because stand-up comedy was still a relatively new art form in the 1970s, stand-up shows often featured comedy teams and improv comedy groups. The Original Comedy Rangers performed at Zanies during its opening week. Pictured from left to right are (first row) Jeff Michalski and John Axness; (second row) Tony Papaleo; (third row) Stew Oleson, Craig Brolley, and Jim Fay. Of the members, many continued their entertainment careers. Michalski and Fay enjoyed successful stints at Second City. Oleson switched to stand-up, performing at night while working as an assistant state's attorney in Chicago during the day; the Moline native also hosted a travel show that won 13 Telly Awards. Fay passed away in 1987. (Courtesy of Zanies.)

After a move to Los Angeles in the 1990s, Jimmy Pardo was no longer among Chicago's best-kept secrets as he began performing on *The Tonight Show with Jay Leno* and *The Late Late Show with Craig Ferguson*. He also appeared on *Monk*, *That '70s Show*, and *Becker*, as well as in the movie *The Godfather of Green Bay*. (Courtesy of Zanies.)

Influenced by Shelley Berman, among others, Chicago's Jeff Garlin toured as a stand-up before breaking out in his role as Jeff Greene on HBO's *Curb Your Enthusiasm*. While living in Chicago, Garlin once rented a small room in his apartment to Conan O'Brien. The two soon began entertaining each other in "Wild Blue Yonder," a mock late-night television show that they staged in their apartment. (Courtesy of Bill Brady.)

Building on his success, Pardo was hired to be Conan O'Brien's audience warm-up, first on *The Tonight Show* and then on *Conan* on TBS. The move soon expanded, with Pardo providing content for O'Brien's website and appearing in some of the show's sketches. When not performing, Pardo hosts the podcast *Never Not Funny*, which was voted by iTunes and *USA Today* as one of the top podcasts of 2006 and 2007. (Both, courtesy of Jimmy Pardo.)

After wanting to be a comedian since he heard a George Carlin album at age 10, Paul Gilmartin began performing stand-up in 1987 at the Comedy Cottage in Merrillville, Indiana. The South Holland native quickly rose through the comedy ranks, appearing on *Comedy Central Presents* and *The Late Late Show with Craig Ferguson*. From 1995 to 2011, Gilmartin cohosted TBS's *Dinner and a Movie*. In 2011, Gilmartin began hosting his own podcast, *The Mental Illness Happy Hour*. (Courtesy of Zanies.)

Before he wrote, directed, produced, and starred in 1987's *Hollywood Shuffle*, a satirical film about black actors in Hollywood, Chicago-born Robert Townsend performed locally as an actor and stand-up. Townsend has worked behind the scenes on numerous television shows and films, including the 2009 documentary *Why We Laugh: Black Comedians on Black Comedy*, for which he served as a co-executive producer. (Courtesy of Zanies.)

In 1982, John DaCosse's first try at stand-up led to an immediate booking at the Comedy Cottage, but it was not until he opened for Howie Mandel at Who's on 1st two years later that DaCosse realized "how cool this business was." Raised in Maywood, Illinois, DaCosse has appeared on Comedy Central's *Stand-Up Stand-Up* and opened for Jay Leno and George Lopez. (Courtesy of Zanies.)

Another sharp Chicago comedian who has flown under the hometown radar, Anthony Griffith was raised on Chicago's South Side and began performing stand-up in college. By 1992, he had appeared on *The Tonight Show* four times and, as of 2014, had made more 25 appearances on national television. (Courtesy of Zanies.)

An admirer of stand-up as a kid, Pete Schwaba did not pursue comedy until he went to college at DePaul University, where he won the College Comedy Hot Shots of Chicago contest. The finals were held at Zanies, where Schwaba waited in the green room with professional comedians including Anthony Griffith, who Schwaba recalls "was having a Chicago Italian beef sandwich between shows, [and] I remember thinking, someday I want to be in his position: a working comic just hanging out in the green room at Zanies between shows." Later, Schwaba wrote, produced, directed, and starred in *The Godfather of Green Bay*. The 2005 comedy featured Lauren Holly (below, left) as Schwaba's love interest and costarred Chicago comedians Steve Seagren, Mike Toomey, and Jimmy Pardo. (Left, courtesy of Zanies; below, courtesy of Pete Schwaba.)

Chicago native Pete Schwaba (far left) played Joe Keegan in *The Godfather of Green Bay*. Other cast members include, from left to right, Lauren Holly, Thomas Lennon, Lance Barber, Tracy Thorpe, and Steve Seagren. (Courtesy of Pete Schwaba.)

A former prep sportswriter, Mike Siegel has appeared on *The Late Late Show* with Craig Kilborn and HBO's *Comedy Showcase* with Louie Anderson. Siegel also had a recurring role on the television show *JAG* and appeared in the movies *Traffic* and *The Godfather of Green Bay*. (Courtesy of Bill Brady.)

A multitalented performer who starred as Bob Uecker's reserved sidekick Monte in the *Major League* movies, Skip Griparis incorporates traditional stand-up, music, and impressions in his act. Griparis learned to play piano and saxophone at a young age and toured with Olivia Newton-John's band as a musician and singer for four years. (Courtesy of Zanies.)

With a degree in agriculture from the University of Illinois and a master's degree from the Medill School of Journalism at Northwestern University, Taylor Mason does not have the type of background one would expect for a ventriloquist. Mason, whose act also features music and traditional stand-up, performed regularly at Zanies in the early 1980s before he moved to New York City. (Courtesy of Zanies.)

A stand-up since 1986, Tony Boswell has performed more than 5,000 shows in 42 states and 9 countries. Once, while performing in a bowling alley's lounge, someone ran in during Boswell's show and yelled, "Steve's got a perfect game going on lane 12!"—half the audience left to watch. Boswell was also the opening act for the taping of an HBO special featuring Bill Hicks. (Courtesy of Bill Brady.)

Comical voices and facial expressions have been a staple of Jimmy McHugh's act since he first took the stage at the Comedy Cottage in 1978. He also performed sports humor, with the *Chicago Sun-Times* reporting that McHugh "delivers some of the funniest sports material." McHugh has performed on the *Oprah Winfrey Show* and has appeared on stand-up shows on Comedy Central, HBO, and MTV. (Courtesy of Bill Brady.)

When others moved west to be on television, longtime stand-up Mike Preston hunkered down in Chicago's northwest suburbs and created *Psycho Babble*, a cable access television program that is part variety show, part talk show, and all comedy. Since *Psycho Babble* premiered in 2002, a laundry list of celebrities have appeared on the show, including Gene Simmons and Tony Curtis. (Courtesy of Zanies.)

Chicago comedians are not shy about appearing as reoccurring characters on Preston's show. Pictured below are, from left to right, Mike Toomey, Bob Jay, Marge Tackes, host Mike Preston, and Jimmy McHugh. This episode was filmed live at Zanies in St. Charles in 2010. (Courtesy of Mike Preston.)

When not cohosting or on assignment for *Psycho Babble*, veteran comedienne Marge Tackes tours the country with Susan Smith to perform as "The Untamed Shrews," a no-holds-barred comedy duo. (Courtesy of Bill Brady.)

Comedian T.R. Benker performs as Lance Vegas (left) as Marge Tackes (center) and Mike Preston watch. (Courtesy of Mike Preston.)

A Milwaukee transplant who once tried out for the Kansas City Royals baseball team, Dobie Maxwell started performing stand-up at the Comedy Cottage in 1983 and was touring the Midwest two years later. Overall, the comic known as "Mister Lucky" has performed in 48 states and Canada. In 2010, Maxwell appeared on *The Late Late Show with Craig Ferguson.* (Courtesy of Bill Brady.)

Born in Detroit, political satirist Tim Slagle settled in Chicago in the mid-1980s, where he became a regular at Zanies. In 2000, he produced and starred in the short-lived Minneapolis television show *The Mudslingers Ball* with comedians Lewis Black and Will Durst, among others. (Courtesy of Zanies.)

90

From Chicago's Canaryville neighborhood, Kevin Naughton was known for catchphrase, "Don't Make Me Snap!" The expression was a by-product of an angry and edgy act in which Naughton would riff on everyday encounters like trips to the supermarket, which Naughton dubbed his "obstacle course of ignorance." (Courtesy of Bill Brady.)

Chicagoan T.P. Mulrooney began his comedy career on the East Coast, working in clubs in and around New York City and Washington, DC. After taking up golf some years later, Mulrooney has carved out a niche as "the Golf Comic" and has performed at more than 400 corporate and charity golf events, including the Ryder Cup and the Masters. (Courtesy of Zanies.)

Soon after leaving graduate school at Northwestern University in 1995, Chicago native Patti Vasquez began pursuing her lifelong love of stand-up and started emceeing at Zanies, working her way up to headliner. Vasquez has since starred in a number of one-woman shows, including *Mamacita* and *Lipstick Mom*, and appeared on the television reality show *My Life is a Joke*. (Courtesy of Patti Vasquez.)

South Sider Pat McGann started his career in 2008 and is the creator and host of the Chicago WTTW television show *The Chicago Stand-Up Project*, which features local celebrities trying stand-up with the backing of Chicago comedians. Here, Father Tom Hurley (left) gets some last minute advice from McGann before taking the stage. (Courtesy of Pat McGann.)

Five

WHO'S ON 1ST

Chicago's comedy clubs attracted more than budding comedians. They also attracted regular customers like John Hallinan, a regional controller for American Building Maintenance Company. One night at the Comedy Cottage, Hallinan made an important decision that went beyond applauding comedians. He approached Denise Mix, the Cottage's assistant manager, and proposed a business venture: if Mix found an empty space, he would finance a comedy club that she could manage.

Unsure of the seriousness of Hallinan's plan, Mix kept the proposal to herself until word got out, and Ted Holum, co-owner of the Comedy Womb, was brought on board as a third partner. With everything finalized except a club location, Holum phoned his former manager, Ken Voss. As the founder and editor of *Illinois Entertainer* magazine, Voss knew where the vacant stages were, so he suggested Holum check out Rock Gardens, a former rock club in Elmhurst.

Hallinan's plan came to fruition in April 1982, when Who's on 1st comedy club introduced former *Smothers Brothers Comedy Hour* cast member Pat Paulsen as its first headliner. Initially, business was slow, but as word spread, so did the club's popularity, especially among comics. For the club's second anniversary, Jay Leno headlined.

For Chicago comedians, rubbing elbows with prominent comedians was another perk to having excelled for Holum at the Comedy Womb.

"The young guys [at the Womb], once they got good, could emcee at 'Who's,'" Holum said. "When they got a little better, they could be the opening act. The Womb was kind of like a training ground."

The extended stage time was also beneficial, as Who's on 1st adopted the growing trend of hiring just an emcee, opener, and headliner. The idea originated after larger portions of each show's budget was being reserved for headliners.

In the early days, crowds regularly flooded the 200-seat club; sadly, so did Salt Creek, the body of water located just west of the club. Frustrated, Who's on 1st's owners finally closed the club in 1992. Hallinan passed away in 2004 at age 72.

In 1993, Fun Seekers comedy club opened in the space and, under the guidance of two different owners, Dick Senese and then Barry Manheim, lasted until 1998.

Located near the intersection of North Avenue and Route 83 in Elmhurst, Who's on 1st comedy club was set back from the street and situated between two restaurants, one of which was the Golden Pheasant. (Courtesy of Denise Mix.)

In later years, the layout of the property flip-flopped. A strip mall (right) was built in the space where Who's on 1st's customers parked, and strip mall customers now park where the comedy club once stood. (Photograph by Vince Vieceli.)

As the first full-time comedy club in the western suburbs of Chicago, Who's on 1st created a loyal customer base that allowed them to bring in up-and-coming comedians like Jay Leno, shown here with club manager Denise Mix. (Courtesy of Denise Mix.)

Minnesota native Louie Anderson headlined the club in 1986, the same year the iconic Chicago movie *Ferris Bueller's Day Off* was released. Anderson played a delivery man in the film. (Courtesy of Denise Mix.)

Though her sitcom would not debut for another two years, Roseanne Barr (left) was well known in and out of the stand-up circuit when she stopped by Who's on 1st in 1986. Barr needed little encouragement from Denise Mix (right) to do a guest set for the Who's on 1st faithful. (Courtesy of Denise Mix.)

Banks, uncertain about comedy clubs in general, were reluctant to extend credit to the owners of Who's on 1st when they first opened. To help pay for its marquee, comedy magician The Amazing Johnathan did a benefit show at the club. (Courtesy of Denise Mix.)

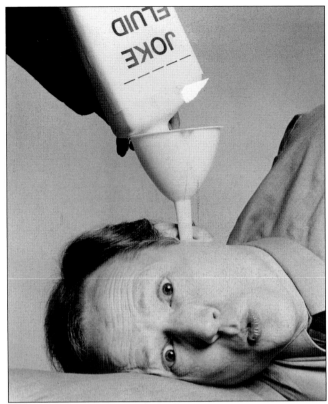

Tim Cavanagh's promotional photographs are something people looked forward to, like a new release from a favorite author or band. The former high school teacher turned national headliner has released three comedy albums featuring many of the song parodies that have made him a Dr. Demento favorite and a regular guest on the syndicated radio program *The Bob & Tom Show*. Cavanagh has appeared on Comedy Central's *Stand-Up Stand-Up* and George Schlatter's comedy special. (Both, courtesy of Bill Brady.)

"Where do I know him from?" is what audiences typically ask when Matt Kissane takes the stage. Since first appearing at Who's on 1st in 1989, the Lombard native has carved out a second career as actor, landing a variety of commercials spots. Behind the camera, Kissane has directed music videos for Enuff Z'nuff and Slitheryn and produced a documentary about Cheap Trick. (Courtesy of Bill Brady.)

Considered one of Boston's top comedians, Ken Rogerson (left) learned some of his craft while living in Chicago in the early 1980s. Rogerson, pictured with Dale Irvin, was also a member of the Comedy Rangers and appeared in the films *Fever Pitch* and *There's Something About Mary*. (Courtesy of Denise Mix.)

Upon finding a trio of mannequin heads in the trash outside of a beauty shop, Leo Benvenuti engineered the mouths so that they could move and attended a Halloween party as the Mills Brothers, a vocal quartet he came to idolize in high school. At the urging of others, Benvenuti made the joke part of *The Steve and Leo Show,* lip-syncing to the song "Glow Worm." (Courtesy of Marlene Patterson.)

Before the use of props became something of a stigma in the mid-1990s, comedians were more open to incorporating variety into their acts, particularly as a means of spoofing or satirizing a subject. Mark Roberts's act featured a bit with a dummy he called "Little Elvis." (Courtesy of Denise Mix.)

On Sunday nights, Who's on 1st offered an improv comedy night that was hosted by Steve Rudnick (right) and Leo Benvenuti. Shows were loosely structured and featured a handful of regulars, including Bob Odenkirk, plus willing comedians like Jeff Garlin. (Courtesy of Marlene Patterson.)

Some of Chicago's best improv actors starred in the Sunday shows, too. Tom Gianas went on to write and produce at *Saturday Night Live*. Elmhurst native Ken Campbell starred in the 1990s sitcom *Herman's Head* and played "Max" in the movie *Armageddon*. Pictured here are, from left to right, Gianas, Leo Benvenuti, A.J. Lentini, Campbell, Steve Rudnick, and unidentified. (Courtesy of Marlene Patterson.)

Lew Schneider was another Sunday night regular. Originally from Boston, Schneider moved to Chicago in the 1980s, where he worked as a stand-up comedian and studied improv comedy at Second City. Schneider later wrote for and produced *Everybody Loves Raymond*, for which he won two Emmy Awards. (Courtesy of Marlene Patterson.)

Comedian and impressionist Jeff Kelch began his career in 1980 in his native Ohio and moved to Chicago in 1984. Aside from clubs, Kelch performed at the Holiday Star Plaza Theater and opened for numerous acts, including Chicago and Eddie Murphy. In 1991, Kelch stopped touring, and as of 2014, he was an executive with Heritage Werks, a national archival services firm with offices in suburban Chicago. (Courtesy of Bill Brady.)

In the late 1980s and early 1990s, Chicago's emerging comedy community was very close-knit. Who's on 1st regularly hosted parties for comics, staff, and guests; at Who's, these arrangements were also made possible thanks to outside seating and a brick grill. Above, the exterior of the club is decorated for Christmas. The revelers below include, from left to right, Pat Duax, Dave Grier, Vince Maranto, unidentified, Kevin Lampe, and Ted Holum. (Both, courtesy of Denise Mix.)

Who's on 1st server Paula Komada works the grill in the above photograph, while Pat Duax's Good Humor truck is in the background. Pictured below are, from left to right, server Nancy Haggerty, bartender Robin Capparelli, server Mary Tiffin, and legal counsel Kevin Mix, brother of Denise Mix. (Both, courtesy of Denise Mix.)

The Salt Creek, located just west of Who's on 1st, flowed east for 11 miles and emptied into the Des Plaines River near the Comedy Womb in Lyons. In the mid-1980s, it was not unusual for certain sections of the Salt Creek to flood nearby homes and businesses. In the image below, the white, horizontal mark on the stage curtains shows how high the waters rose during one flood. (Both, courtesy of Denise Mix.)

Six

THE FUNNY BONE

As stand-up comedy grew popular in Chicago, the same thing was happening in other cities, and it was not long before the owners of the nationally known Funny Bone clubs began to think about expanding.

Owned by Gerald Kubach and Mitch Kutash, the Funny Bone operated two clubs in St. Louis, as well as several other cities, when it was presented with an opportunity in the mid-1980s. Through a business connection, Kubach learned that the Sheraton-Walden Hotel in Schaumburg—a suburb of Chicago—housed a 300-seat, tiered showroom that was only used for breakfast and lunch service and the occasional private party. The set-up deviated from the strip malls the Funny Bone traditionally targeted, but nonetheless, the deal was too enticing to reject.

To oversee the club, Kubach and Kutash selected Bert Borth, a young St. Louis comedian who had also used his advertising background to assist the chain.

"Business was booming in that location from day one," Borth said of the club, which opened in September 1986. "We had an advertising budget of $2,000 per week that we split with the hotel, so we were running a lot of radio spots and promotions as well as regular print ads in the *Chicago Tribune* and the *Daily Herald*. This was something that none of the other clubs in Chicago had done."

For the club's opening weekend, Borth warmed up the crowd for coheadliners John Riggi, a Cincinnati native who later moved to Chicago, and Houston comedian Mike Vance. Later headliners included Drew Carey, who made his *Tonight Show* debut the same week he was scheduled to appear at the Schaumburg and Naperville Funny Bones, and Denver comic Matthew Berry, who later became ESPN's senior fantasy sports analyst.

"That is the one thing the Funny Bone did that was ahead of the pack as far as comedy clubs were concerned," Borth said, "they were the first to bring in different touring acts each week, mostly from the East and West Coasts."

By 1993, a corporate restructuring within the Funny Bone and a change in hotel ownership had doomed the club. Oddly, its significance grew in later years, as fewer hotels contained lounges or bars where live comedy could be staged. Even as the Schaumburg location closed, the Funny Bone was not done with Chicago—their Naperville club was just taking shape.

St. Louis native Bert Borth was the first manager of the Schaumburg Funny Bone. For Borth, a young comedian, the position was particularly attractive because it also allowed him to perform at other Funny Bone locations throughout the Midwest. Later, Borth managed the chain's Naperville club before opening Comedy Comedy in Lisle and then Aurora. (Courtesy of Bert Borth.)

To promote the club, the Funny Bone relied heavily on radio advertising. Here, Chicago comedian Stew Oleson (left) records a radio spot with Bert Borth. (Courtesy of Bert Borth.)

Though he's an accomplished magician, Syracuse native Jeff Altman (right) is more well known for his stand-up comedy (and his Jack Benny impressions). Altman is pictured with Funny Bone manager Bert Borth. (Courtesy of Bert Borth.)

Long before Bill Maher (right) was selling out thousand-seat theaters, the New York comedian regularly performed at the Funny Bones in Schaumburg and Naperville. Maher (right) is pictured with Bert Borth. (Courtesy of Bert Borth.)

Nearly 10 years after appearing as a regular on the television game show *Make Me Laugh*, Los Angeles comic Vic Dunlop (center) remained a crowd favorite, often selling out his performances at the Funny Bone. Pictured with Dunlop are Funny Bone managers Bert (left) and Janet Borth. (Courtesy of Bert Borth.)

The Funny Bone did not only hire headliners from out of town. Chicago-born comedian and actor Rondell Sheridan (right, pictured with Bert Borth) was a club favorite and costarred on the Disney Channel's *That's So Raven*, as well as the show's spin-off, *Cory in the House*. (Courtesy of Bert Borth.)

Ohio native John Riggi coheadlined the Schaumburg Funny Bone's first weekend along with Mike Vance. Riggi later moved into television writing and producing, serving as co-executive producer for *30 Rock*, *Will & Grace*, *The Bernie Mac Show*, and *The Larry Sanders Show*.

Rhode Island native Poppy Champlin moved to Chicago to study at Second City and transitioned to stand-up, a move that put her on the fast track to becoming a headliner, including for a few weeks at the Schaumburg Funny Bone. Champlin is the producer of the Queer Queens of Qomedy tour. (Courtesy of Bill Brady.)

A veteran comedian who was opened for Jerry Seinfeld and Steven Wright, Tim Clue is also a motivational speaker and playwright, cowriting the hit comedic play *Leaving Iowa*. (Courtesy of Zanies.)

To say Spike Manton is comfortable behind a microphone is an understatement. The longtime comic spent three years hosting sports radio shows on ESPN Radio and six years on various FM programs. Manton also cowrote the play *Leaving Iowa*. (Courtesy of Bill Brady.)

Although they are not a comedy team, brothers Lenny (above) and Mike (right) Schmidt are both comedians. Lenny, inspired to become a comedian after seeing Sam Kinison and Carl LaBove at the Comedy Store, first started doing comedy at the Improv in Sherman Oaks, California, in 1988 before returning and performing locally. Lenny has appeared on *Castle*, *True Blood*, and *Big Love*, among other shows. Mike Schmidt also started comedy in Los Angeles and bounced between cities. In addition to appearing in *BASEketball* and *Malcolm in the Middle*, Mike produces his own podcast, *The 40-Year-Old Boy*. (Both, courtesy of Bill Brady; above photograph by William Cramp, right photograph by Denny Weber.)

Although the names on the sign have changed over the years, the building in Schaumburg (pictured above) where the Chicago area's first Funny Bone opened has remained a hotel, operating under the Best Western name as recently as 2014. Years later, the Funny Bone opened a club in suburban Naperville before pulling out of the Chicago market completely in 1999. Club manager Bert Borth then opened a comedy club called Comedy Comedy in a hotel in suburban Lisle before relocating to Water Payton's Roundhouse (below) in Aurora. Comedy shows were held in the converted transportation center until 2011, when the club relocated to Aurora. (Both photographs by Vince Vieceli.)

Seven

THE COMEDY BOOM AND COLLAPSE

The massive influx of full-time comedy clubs attracted freshmen comedians who challenged upperclassmen for stage time, and as a result, the mushrooming talent pool allowed bookers to rotate their lineups. The resulting combination of available comics, entrepreneurial minds, and a new demand for comedy shows outside of the Comedy Cottage and the Comedy Womb led to the expansion of clubs offering one-nighters. Though this made an impact, the ramifications paled in comparison to the comedy boom, a blast that would eventually contribute to the demise of all but two of Chicago's original comedy clubs.

Between 1985 and 1988, the number of comedy clubs in Chicago swelled from the original five—Comedy Cottage, Comedy Womb, Barrel of Laughs, Zanies Comedy Club, and Who's on 1st—to 16. Expansion occurred from within as both Ed Hellenbrand and Zanies added second clubs (in Roselle and Mount Prospect, respectively), and Jay Berk operated Last Laugh, located in the original Comedy Cottage location, and a second club in Merrillville, Indiana.

Otherwise, outside interests sparked the expansion, as New York's Catch a Rising Star opened two locations (in Chicago and Oak Brook), and Budd Friedman's Improv (Chicago) and the Funny Bone (Schaumburg) each opened one club. Other additions included the Funny Firm (Chicago), Wacko's (Berwyn), and the Comedy Club (Northbrook).

Clubs continued to open and fold—or change names, owners, or buildings—with notables including Chaplin's, a Detroit-based 600-seat flop that lasted six weeks, and the Los Angeles–based Laugh Factory (Aurora). Other local additions included the Funny Firm (Chicago), Wacko's (Berwyn), the Comedy Club (Northbrook), and K.J. Riddles (Orland Park), which survived and continues today as Riddles Comedy Club in south suburban Alsip.

In the end, too many clubs, a weak economy, and competition for the entertainment dollar contributed to a comedy collapse in the mid-1990s.

Even as demand for comedy began to cool, Chicago's stand-ups were talented enough to support the multitude of clubs that set up shop. For instance, when 10 clubs booked a local feature act and emcee for the week, 20 Chicago comedians got calls. Many of these comics have already been featured within this book; still more are on the following pages.

Friends and talented musicians Pat Hall (above, right) and Dave Grier formed a musical comedy team in 1986 after comedian Jim Wiggins, who was a friend of Hall's, needed a favor. With the comedy boom underway, Wiggins had convinced Durty Nellie's, a small music venue in suburban Palatine, to offer stand-up comedy. For the club's first show, Wiggins had booked his long-time pal George Carlin. "Could you open for Carlin?" Wiggins asked Hall, who then called on Grier, and their "A Coupla Fat Guys" comedy team was born. After the Carlin show, the pair honed their act and expanded to other clubs and venues, opening for Robert Wuhl, Lewis Black, and Paul Reiser, among others. The duo later formed the semi-serious Coupla Fat Guys band. Pat Hall passed away in 2010. In the photograph at left, T.S. Henry Webb (left), Grier (center), and Hall perform at Nellie's. (Both, courtesy of and photographs by Monica Grier.)

With singers, dancers, magicians, acrobats, a pipe organ, and hostesses on roller skates (as well as performers, sometimes, as shown in the image at right), Sally's Stage was not exactly a comedy club, but it was a venue where comedians like Bob Rumba could gain stage time. (Courtesy of Bob Rumba.)

Some nights, anything could—and would—happen at the Stay Out All Night Disco, where stand-up comedy shows often began after 2:00 a.m. Here, a woman wearing a halter leotard gets a reaction from the "Marx Brothers," portrayed by, from top to bottom, Bob Rumba (Groucho), Ron Gandy (Chico), and Steve Marmer (Harpo). (Courtesy of Bob Rumba.)

Not every Chicago one-nighter was staged in a restaurant or bar. Bill Gorgo was among several stand-ups hired to perform in Marshall Field's department store for passing customers in 1989. (Courtesy of Bill Gorgo.)

Although Bit O' Magic was known as magic club, the Chicago venue also offered a bit of comedy, especially during Saturday afternoon shows for kids. Here, Emo Philips (right) brings a young audience member on stage to join in the act. (Courtesy of the William Cramp estate; photograph by William Cramp.)

Because Dave Orion was underage, his father had to chaperone him when Orion started doing stand-up at the Comedy Womb in 1978. Orion's father came to the club with him until he turned 21. Since then, Orion has opened for Jerry Seinfeld and Tim Allen, and in 1989, he won *Star Search*. (Photograph by William Cramp, courtesy of the William Cramp estate.)

Nick Gaza, mentored by T.P. Mulrooney, he started stand-up in late 1986 at Larry McManus's Comedyland club. Gaza has toured the country, with extended stays in Los Angeles, where he appeared on *The Drew Carey Show*, *Malcolm in the Middle*, *Becker*, *Comedy Central Tough Crowd with Colin Quinn*, *Dharma & Greg*, *Profiler*, *The Pretender*, and *Grace Under Fire*. (Courtesy of Bill Brady.)

A former circus clown who also studied at Second City, Chicago native Chas Elstner first began performing stand-up in the 1980s and has since produced two comedy albums and appeared four times on *An Evening at the Improv*. (Courtesy of Bill Brady; photograph by William Cramp.)

Raised in Kentucky until he was 14, Hal Sparks moved with his family to Chicago and, in 1987, won the Chicago's Funniest Teenager stand-up contest sponsored by the *Chicago Sun-Times*. In 2000, Sparks was cast as Michael Novotny in the Showtime show *Queer as Folk*. (Courtesy of Zanies.)

After being whisked off the Comedy Womb stage by pals A.J. Lentini (left) and Kevin Lampe (right), comedian Al Altur has never been seen or heard from again. Actually, while moonlighting as a comic, Altur worked as a graphic designer for the Environmental Protection Agency. In the 1990s, Altur moved west and joined Lentini Design. (Courtesy of the William Cramp estate; photograph by William Cramp.)

Veteran comedian Al Katz has appeared on numerous television shows, including the *Showtime Comedy Club Network* and *The Oprah Winfrey Show*, as well as stand-up shows on HBO and Comedy Central. (Courtesy of the William Cramp estate; photograph by William Cramp.)

Paul Frisbie got on a comedy stage for the first time while he was in college—and at the bar he owned, the Alley Cat, which was located on campus at the University of Illinois at Urbana-Champaign. Frisbie hosted an amateur comedy night and soon graduated to headliner status. Frisbie has appeared in numerous television commercials throughout the Midwest. (Courtesy of Paul Frisbie.)

Props, music, and merriment were always elements of Bill Kraze's show. (Courtesy of the William Cramp estate; photograph by William Cramp.)

Indiana native Lisa Bonnice moved to Chicago and added to the city's deep pool of talent during the comedy boom. In 2013, Bonnice coauthored *Fear of Our Father: A True Story of Abuse, Murder, and Family Ties*, a true crime book. (Courtesy of Bill Brady.)

Raised in Wabash, Indiana, but drawn to Chicago because of its comedy tradition, Michael Palascak studied at Second City and iO before trying stand-up. Palascak has appeared on *Late Show with David Letterman*, *The Tonight Show with Jay Leno*, and *The Late Late Show with Craig Ferguson*. (Courtesy of Bill Brady.)

Former newspaper and television news reporter Greg Schwem saw an opportunity to pursue a hobby when a comedy club opened near his Florida apartment. His subsequent rise up the comedy ladder coincided with a move north to his hometown of Chicago. An in-demand headliner, Schwem signed on as a syndicated columnist for Tribune Media Services in 2012. (Courtesy of Bill Brady; photograph by Denny Weber.)

After finding improv comedy to be a "dead end" for her, Rhonda Cohn switched to stand-up and has since opened for Jackie Mason. (Courtesy of Bill Brady; photograph by William Cramp.)

Some Chicago comedians left us too soon; others left us with a lot. Pictured above are Dan Flatley (right) and Bob Thomas (left). Below is Eddie Merrill. (Both above, courtesy of Bill Brady; below, courtesy of the William Cramp estate, photograph by William Cramp.)

40 Years of Chicago Comedy Clubs & One-Nighters (1972 to 2012)

*Abbey, Chicago
*Agustano's, Dolton
*Allgauer's Northbrook
All Jokes Aside
*Apple Pub, Chicago
* Big John's Distillery, Chicago
Barrel of Laughs, Oak Lawn
Bit O'Magic, Chicago
*Bourbon Street, Saint Charles
*Byfield's, Chicago
Catch a Rising, Chicago
Catch A Rising, Oak Brook
Chaplins, Chicago
Clout Club, Chicago
The Comedy Club, Northbrook
Comedy Klik, Chicago
Comedy Cellar, Lombard
Comedy College, Rosemont
Comedy Comedy, Aurora
Comedy Comedy, Lisle
Comedy Cottage, Merrillville, IN
Comedy Cottage, Rosemont
Comedy Cottage West, Roselle
Comedy Hut, Chicago
Comedy Womb, Lyons
Cotton Club, Chicago
*Danny Boy's, Saint Charles
*Doc Weeds, Chicago
Double Exposure, Oak Brook
*Frigate's, Crystal Lake
Funny Bone, Naperville
Funny Bone, Schaumburg
Funny Firm, Chicago
Fun Seekers, Elmhurst
Great Lakes Naval Base
*Griswold's, Crestwood
*Groucho's, Chicago
*Houdini's, Oak Forest
Improv, Chicago

Jokes and Notes, Chicago
*Kingston's Mines, Chicago
Last Laugh, Lisle
Last Laugh, Rosemont
Laugh Factory, Aurora
Le Pub, Chicago
* Lilly's Lounge, Saint Charles
*Lorenzo's, Riverdale
*Michelle's, Crestwood
*Milt Trenniers, Chicago
* Nikko's, Blue Island
*Pickle Barrel, Chicago locations
*Poor Richard's, Gurnee
*Primetime, Arlington Heights
* Puttin' on the Ritz, Lombard
*RG Nostalgia, Channahon
Riddles, Berwyn
Riddles, Orland Park
*Ringside, Elk Grove
*Roar's , Highland Park
Roxy, Chicago
*Sally's Stage, Chicago
The Comedy Club, Schaumburg
*Someplace Else, Park Forest
* Slip's, Dalton
Spices Jazz Bar, Chicago
*Stay Out All Night, Stone Park
The Comedy Club, Northbrook
*Three Stooges, Worth
TNT Comedy Hook, Tinley Park
*Vineyard, Darien
Wacko's, Berwyn
Who's on First, Elmhurst
Zanies, Chicago
Zanies, Mount Prospect
Zanies, Rosemont
Zanies, Saint Charles
Zanies, Vernon Hills

*Denotes one-nighters. Clubs listed my be incomplete due to space.
(Photo of Vince Maranto by William Cramp. Photo courtesy of the William Cramp estate.)

This is a partial list of Chicago-area comedy clubs, where many fantastic comedians performed.

Eight

ALL JOKES ASIDE

When Raymond Lambert returned to Chicago after a business trip in the late 1980s, he carried an unusual souvenir: inspiration. Nearly 18 years after Budd Friedman's Improv club had inspired Dreesen, Lambert was under a similar spell, charmed by an urban-oriented show at Friedman's Los Angeles location.

For the next year, Lambert researched the comedy business and, seeing an underserved market in Chicago's black community, teamed with James Alexander to open All Jokes Aside in 1991. At first, shows were staged in a space rented from an art gallery, with some technical basics reminiscent of those at the Comedy College. Without light boards, All Jokes relied on James Alexander's sister Lori and her boyfriend to illuminate the stage by simultaneously turning on opposing spotlights.

When business boomed, All Jokes hired Mary Lindsey to handle personnel and moved next door to a permanent space; these changes allowed Lambert to focus more on the business. Even with an MBA degree, Lambert required outside help, and Chicago comedian Bernie Mac stepped up.

"What we brought to the table was how to run a business day in and day out. What [Bernie] brought was the knowledge that you get from being in the business for a decade or so. That helped us get up to speed. He sort of taught us the business from a comedian's perspective."

A Chicago native and a stand-up since 1977, Mac broke through 12 years later when he won a national comedy competition at age 32. Offers followed, and soon, Mac was on the fast track to stardom, performing on the Original Kings of Comedy tour, starring in his own sitcom, and appearing in many films, including *Mr. 3000*. Sadly, Mac died in 2008.

Because of the support from Mac, Steve Harvey, and others, All Jokes became the country's most successful black comedy club and was the focus of the award-winning 2012 Showtime documentary *Phunny Business: A Black Comedy*.

In ways similar to what other Chicago comedy clubs had experienced years earlier, All Jokes battled a changing economic climate before closing in 1998. Lambert's efforts to reopen the club in a white neighborhood were met with local resistance, and a new club never materialized.

Born Bernard Jeffrey McCullough, Bernie Mac got his start on Chicago's South Side before breaking through when he won the Miller Lite Comedy Search—a national comedy contest—in 1990. Mac scored again as one of the Original Kings of Comedy and then with *The Bernie Mac Show,* for which he received two Emmy nominations. He also appeared in several films, including *Ocean's Eleven.* Mac passed away in 2008. (Courtesy of Vince Vieceli.)

Dubbed "The Stress Reliever," George Willborn has brought the laughs since first taking the stage in 1987. For many years, Willborn served as the emcee at All Jokes Aside; he later moved on to Mary Lindsey's Jokes and Notes comedy club in Chicago. Willborn's career extended to radio, where he cohosted the nationally syndicated *Michael Baisden Show* for 10 years and is now part of the *Doug Banks Radio Show.* (Courtesy of Zanies.)

A founding member of Chicago comedy trio Mary Wong, which also included Lance Crouther and Tim Miller, Ali LeRoi made a name for his himself as a stand-up before making an even bigger name for himself in Hollywood. LeRoi is the cocreator and executive producer of the comedy *Everybody Hates Chris* and the creator and executive producer of sitcom *Are We There Yet?* He won an Emmy in 1999, when he was a writer for *The Chris Rock Show.* (Courtesy of Zanies.)

Damon Williams served as the emcee for All Jokes Aside's Wednesday night open mic night and later at the TNT Comedy Hook in suburban Lansing. Since then, Williams has appeared as the opening act for the Original Kings of Comedy tour and had his own one-hour special on BET's *ComicView.* He has also hosted several episodes of the legendary *Showtime at the Apollo.* (Courtesy of Zanies.)

DISCOVER THOUSANDS OF LOCAL HISTORY BOOKS FEATURING MILLIONS OF VINTAGE IMAGES

Arcadia Publishing, the leading local history publisher in the United States, is committed to making history accessible and meaningful through publishing books that celebrate and preserve the heritage of America's people and places.

Find more books like this at
www.arcadiapublishing.com

Search for your hometown history, your old stomping grounds, and even your favorite sports team.